D0359656

THE HUNTING GROUND

THE INSIDE STORY OF SEXUAL ASSAULT ON AMERICAN COLLEGE CAMPUSES

KIRBY DICK AND **AMY ZIERING**

EDITED BY CONSTANCE MATTHIESSEN

Hot Books

Hot Books may be purchased in bulk at special discounts for sales promotion, corporate gifts, fund-raising, or educational purposes. Special editions can also be created to specifications. For details, contact the Special Sales Department, Skyhorse Publishing, 307 West 36th Street, 11th Floor, New York, NY 10018 or info@skyhorsepublishing.com.

Hot Books® and Skyhorse Publishing® are registered trademarks of Skyhorse Publishing, Inc.®, a Delaware corporation.

Visit our website at www.hotbookspress.com.

10 9 8 7 6 5 4 3 2 1

Library of Congress Cataloging-in-Publication Data is available on file.

Cover design by Brian Peterson
Cover photo credit Richard Davis

ISBN: 978-1-5107-0574-6
Ebook ISBN: 978-1-5107-0578-4

Printed in the United States of America

Contents

Introduction

by Constance Matthiessen

The Hunting Ground, the powerful documentary by filmmakers Kirby Dick and Amy Ziering, begins with exuber-
ant video clips of high school seniors learning that they've been
accepted by their top-choice colleges. As "Pomp and Circumstance" surges in the background, one girl's face goes from dread
to stunned joy, another dissolves in tears, a third screams and
leaps to her feet, joining her family in a giddy dance around the
dining room.

It's a dream most parents cherish: sending their child to college. The dream features erudite professors, inspiring classes, and
friendships to last a lifetime—all set against a backdrop of stately
buildings and quads shaded by graceful trees.

On its face, Annie Clark's experience at the University of North
Carolina, Chapel Hill, is one every parent would wish for their
child. "I really had a good time there," she recalls early in the film. "I
learned a lot. I loved my professors. The first few weeks I made some
of my best friends, and we're still really close to this day."

Clark, an athlete and North Carolina native, has a round,
open face and a 1,000-watt smile. But her smile fades and her face
tightens as she finishes, almost matter-of-factly, "But two of us were
sexually assaulted before classes even started."

Campus Epidemic

The Hunting Ground tells the stories of dozens of students whose college experience is marred by sexual assault. The film's director, Kirby Dick, and producer, Amy Ziering, are the team that made the documentary *The Invisible War*, an exposé of sexual assault in the military that sparked national outrage, won two Emmy Awards, a Peabody Award, and was nominated for an Academy Award. That film compelled the Pentagon to change policies and was the catalyst for dozens of major reforms passed by Congress and signed into law.

When the filmmakers screened *The Invisible War* at colleges and universities, students repeatedly approached them to talk about sexual violence on their campuses. Dick and Ziering heard so many disturbing stories that they shelved the project they were working on and started making *The Hunting Ground* instead. What followed was two years of in-depth investigative work. Along with their team, they visited dozens of campuses, conducted hundreds of interviews, and tracked a fledgling movement of courageous student activists. The result is a powerful and frightening portrait of sexual violence on campuses across the country—from party schools to the most exclusive bastions of the Ivy League.

The statistics are stunning: More than 20 percent of women and more than 5 percent of men who attend college are sexually assaulted.

Fraternities and Athletics

What's behind this widespread sexual violence? *The Hunting Ground* highlights two fixtures of campus life often associated with sexual assaults: fraternities and athletics.

Fraternities, which today are the center of the social scene at many colleges, are also the setting for many sexual assaults at colleges around the country. While some fraternities foster a spirit of community and inclusiveness that benefits their members and their schools, others perpetuate a macho "bro" culture that encourages binge drinking, misogynistic attitudes, and a pack mentality. This fierce loyalty among fraternity members often works to keep sexual assault cases under wraps, so it's difficult to say how many attacks occur at college fraternities each year, but, according to insurance reports, sexual assaults comprise the second-highest number of claims against fraternities.

College athletes have been linked to a number of highly-publicized campus assaults; a recent notable case is the accusations of rape against Florida State's quarterback Jameis Winston. While the vast majority of athletes would never assault anyone and are horrified by these crimes, research shows that a small minority of athletes (4 percent) commit a disproportionately high number of assaults (19 percent). In many of these cases, the accused athlete is protected by the school and its athletic program because of his importance to the team. As educator and former NFL quarterback Don McPherson tells Dick and Ziering: "I really do believe the vast majority of student athletes are worthy of our admiration. But when you have 18- to 22-year-old kids who are celebrities it creates a toxic environment for a lot of bad behavior. . . . There's a multibillion-dollar industry that wraps around these young men, and if you don't think that they're part of a culture of entitlement, just look at the fanfare that's around college football."

While these three factors play a role in many sexual assaults, they don't explain why these incidents keep occurring at college after college with mind-numbing regularity. Watching *The Hunting Ground,* you realize that campus assaults keep happening because no one is stopping them: Perpetrators keep committing these crimes, quite simply, because they can.

Protecting a Brand

In fact, colleges have done little to stop violence on their campuses, as *The Hunting Ground* (both the film and this book) make clear. When Annie Clark reported her rape to an administrator at the University of North Carolina, the woman replied, "Rape is like a football game, Annie, and if you look back on the game what would you do differently in that situation?"

Other college students report similarly victim-blaming responses from the college administrators they turn to for help:

> *"What were you wearing?"*
> *"What were you drinking? How much did you have to drink?"*
> *"Did you say no? How many times did you say no? How did you say it?"*

Over the course of *The Hunting Ground*, students' assault reports are repeatedly ignored. Or the investigation is stalled. Or the punishment is a perfunctory slap on the wrist. At some colleges, perpetrators have been given ludicrously small fines, or assigned a paper to write. At Stanford University, to give just one example cited in the film, 259 sexual assaults were reported between 1996 and 2013, but only one student faced expulsion. In fact, according to research by *The Huffington Post*, less than one-third of students found guilty of campus sexual assault are expelled. Nationwide, far more students are expelled for cheating than for sexual violence.

A 2014 report commissioned by Senator Claire McCaskill found that countless campus sexual assaults are never even investigated. Researchers found, for example, that 40 percent of colleges had not conducted a single assault investigation in five years. In addition, "More than 21 percent of the nation's largest private institutions conducted fewer investigations than the number of incidents they reported to the Department of Education, with some institutions reporting as many as seven times more incidents of sexual violence than they have investigated," the report found.

Why can't the best minds at the top educational institutions in the country get a handle on this problem?

The fact is that higher education is big business: Total annual cost per student at many colleges now exceeds $60,000 a year. For institutions vying for the best and brightest students, sexual assault represents a public relations nightmare. What parent would elect to send their child to a college—no matter how prestigious—where students were at risk of assault? College administrators have more incentive to brush off assault reports than to aggressively pursue and expel perpetrators. "If a student comes to an administrator with a problem, it's not as if the administrator wants that student to be harmed," explained Claire Bond Potter, a professor at The New School in New York City. "It's not as if the administrator wants the harm to be perpetuated, but their first job is to protect the institution from harm, not the student from harm."

When campus assaults are reported to local law enforcement, results vary widely depending on the incident and the municipality, but many cases are never pursued at all. According to the FBI, for example, just 26 percent of rapes reported to police lead to arrest. Many of these local police departments are under the shadow of the ivory tower in their communities, where the university is often the biggest employer in town.

It's no surprise, then, that 88 percent of women raped on campus do not report the assault (the McCaskill report concluded that rates are even lower, finding that only 5 percent of women report campus rape).

Signs of Change?

Over the last few years, as countless reports of campus assaults have hit the headlines, college students have started to get angry—and to fight back. Demonstrations have flared up at colleges across the country. Columbia University student Emma Sulkowicz carried a mattress to classes and across the stage at graduation to protest the fact that the student she reported as having raped her was not expelled. Three Berkeley women recently filed a federal complaint with the Department of Education and university faculty members and college alumni are adding their voices through organizations like FAR (Faculty Against Rape) and Dartmouth Change, a group of alumni, faculty, parents, and students formed in response to sexual violence and harassment at the college.

UNC students Annie Clark and Andrea Pino are building a national network of student survivors. Their organization, End Rape on Campus, helps survivors develop strategies to increase awareness and pressure on college administrators.

Clark and Pino's primary tool is Title IX, a federal civil rights law that prohibits sex discrimination—including sexual harassment and sexual violence—in education. Clark, Pino, and other activists are using Title IX complaints to pressure colleges to ensure that their campuses are free from sexual harassment and violence.

The issue of campus assault has sparked attention in Washington, DC, as well. The Obama administration launched civil rights investigations at more than 150 colleges and universities. President Obama and Vice President Biden have both spoken out forcefully against sexual violence, and legislation is in the works in Congress.

Backlash from the Skeptics

The exposure of campus sexual assault has triggered backlash, with commentators questioning the epidemic.

The skeptical voices grew even more clamorous after a November 2014 *Rolling Stone* report of a gang rape at a University of Virginia fraternity. The article turned out to be based on flawed reporting and was ultimately retracted. The incident fueled charges of a so-called "rape-hoax culture" on college campuses and critics accused women of lying about being raped to get attention or revenge. But statistics consistently show that false reporting is no more common in incidents of sexual assault or rape than any other crime. (The uproar over the *Rolling Stone* article obscured the University of Virginia's dismal record on campus assault: UVA has never expelled a single student for sexual assault, even when the student admitted the attack.)

Some critics also scoff at the one-in-five figure widely cited as the number of female college students who experience sexual assault during their college career. *Forbes*, for example, called out President Obama for using the statistic in a January 2015 speech: "One in five is a staggeringly high number, one that has led to a moral panic about the issue of sexual assault on campus." But the truth is that national studies over several decades have repeatedly validated the one in five figure. In fact, in just the past year, two major studies by the American Association of Universities and the Department of Justice have put the number at closer to one in four. (See Chapter 7: The Numbers Don't Lie).

Since *The Hunting Ground*'s release, a few critics (most of whom are associated with institutions critiqued in the film) have attempted to disparage it by aggressively trying to discredit the women whose stories are highlighted in the film. These critics have been unable to identify any substantiated factual errors, and their efforts to damage the film or prevent it from being seen have failed. In fact, Jameis Winston's attorneys threatened CNN with a lawsuit if it showed the film, but CNN stood by the film's reporting and aired it on their channel in November 2015. These attacks are in keeping with what the film shows institutions have historically done regarding sexual assault: rather than address these problems at their school, they attack the press and the people who report these crimes.

Despite these attacks, *The Hunting Ground* has had an extraordinary impact on the sexual assault dialogue on college campuses nationwide. The film has screened at more than 1,000 universities, high schools, community centers, and government offices across the country, sparking long-silenced debate and policy change.

The film has had high profile screenings at the White House, Department of Justice, Office of Civil Rights, Department of Education, NCAA, and a number of state legislatures. When Governor Cuomo of New York screened the film for legislators, they swiftly passed "Enough is Enough," a comprehensive new bill aimed at stopping sexual assaults on all New York college campuses. Globally, the film has instigated campaigns to combat sexual violence on campuses. In Australia, the film triggered a country-wide campaign called "The Hunting Ground Australia" to address sexual assault, enlisting nearly all the major universities. At the Academy Awards in February 2016, Vice President Joe Biden introduced Lady Gaga, and "Til It Happens To You," the theme song from the film. Gaga was joined on stage by 50 survivors, many of whom were in the film, and the moving performance was widely considered one of the highlights of the event and one of the most powerful moments in the history of the Academy Awards.

Moral High Ground

Today, at colleges and universities around the country, administrators are scrambling to develop policies and procedures to deal with sexual violence. New sexual assault prevention programs are being unveiled, and disciplinary procedures are being revised and retooled. The University of California announced a comprehensive sexual assault prevention program that is mandatory for students on all 10 UC campuses. Some colleges are imposing new rules on fraternities; others are cracking down on alcohol abuse (Dartmouth and several other schools have banned hard alcohol). Still, it remains to be seen how effective any of these reforms will be, since many college leaders remain unwilling to acknowledge the problem—especially in their own backyards. A 2015 survey of college and university presidents by *Inside Higher Ed* found that less than a third agreed that sexual assault is prevalent at American colleges and universities, and only 6 percent said that it was common at their institution.

Toward that end, psychologist David Lisak challenges college leaders to step up and tackle the problem of sexual assault: "There is this moral high ground in higher education that is sitting vacant," Lisak says. "What I haven't yet seen anywhere . . . is a [college] president who decided that whatever it takes, it has to be done. That's what leadership is."

———

This book tells the story behind this groundbreaking film. We share the accounts of sexual assault survivors and provide an in-depth examination of the case of one of the young women who accused former FSU quarterback Jameis Winston, now a rising NFL star, of rape. We'll learn more from activists in the trenches who are working to increase awareness of these crimes, and often paying a high price for doing so. We'll learn more about the making of *The Hunting Ground*, and the reactions to the film since its premiere. We'll present writers from a variety of backgrounds and perspectives, who weigh in on the issue of sexual assault. Finally, we'll point you to resources so you can learn more about campus sexual assault and what needs to be done to end this epidemic.

1

Voices of Survivors:
Four Stories of Sexual Assault

Much of the power of the *The Hunting Ground* comes from the students who agreed to appear in the film and talk about being sexually assaulted.

The issue is now in the spotlight because of young people like these, who've had the courage to come forward and say, *Yes this is happening. It happened to me.*

Sexual assault survivors not only experience shame and guilt; many develop Post-Traumatic Stress Disorder (PTSD). Symptoms of PTSD include flashbacks, insomnia, anger, anxiety, and depression. Survivors often isolate themselves, avoiding places and situations that remind them of the attack; some relive the assault in frequent, vivid nightmares. They are at higher risk of substance abuse and suicide.

As the medical director of San Francisco General Hospital's Trauma Recovery and Rape Treatment Center, Dr. Laurie Richer sees many sexual assault survivors, including students from Bay Area colleges and universities. Recovery takes time and depends on many factors, according to Richer, including the severity of the attack, and the individual's previous history of trauma. Some people are simply more resilient than others or have more resources, including support from friends and family members.

Richer describes two of her clients, both survivors of campus sexual assault: "I've seen one of these women learn to express herself and move on from it," she said. "The other student can't go to class; she keeps having anxiety episodes. She's falling behind in school. Her world is crashing around her."

Many students who experience sexual assault drop out of college, many lose scholarships, and some become outspoken advocates for change. Almost all move in the world with a wariness they never had before. "All they wanted to do was get a college education," Richer points out. "And now the course of their life has changed: They're living a life that's not at all what they planned."

Hundreds of students came forward to talk to filmmakers Kirby Dick and Amy Ziering for *The Hunting Ground*. These young people represent a broad cross section—including male and female, minority and white, straight and LGBTQ—from colleges across the country. Many of these students make only a brief appearance in the film; others don't appear at all. We've included a few more of their stories here.

Daniel

Daniel (not his real name) was sexually assaulted during his freshman year at one of the most prestigious Ivy League colleges in the country.

It was spring semester and Daniel, who is gay, had recently gone through a breakup. Some friends thought he needed to get out and have some fun, so they took him to a party at an upper-class dorm. It was late in the evening and all of Daniel's friends had left the party when an older student approached him and asked him to dance. The older student became aggressive, and sexually assaulted Daniel. Daniel didn't know what to do: The room was dark, and he was embarrassed and intimidated.

He left as quickly as he could after the assault, and tried to put the incident out of his mind. "For a while I just didn't really acknowledge it," Daniel said. "I kind of thought of it as a bad hookup, because you're taught that assault is something that happens to women."

But Daniel couldn't stop thinking about what happened and how violated he felt. He sought therapy, but he didn't report the incident, even after he learned that his assailant had attacked other students. "I never thought about reporting because I had heard such horror stories from people about what happened if you went to the office that handles this type of situation," he says. "Generally, the assailant was never charged with anything, was never kicked out of school, and typically nothing ever happened. So it's almost a matter of, 'Why am I going to go forward if I'll just be standing out there alone?'"

The college's iconic status and exclusivity also discourages reporting, Daniel says: "It's such a recognizable name and because when you first get the letter you feel so privileged to go there, you don't want to do anything that jeopardizes that." Minority and low-income students are particularly hesitant to speak up: "It's kind of a matter of, 'If I go to the administration, will they even really care because my father didn't donate millions?'"

Males who are sexually assaulted are often reluctant to report, research shows. Men often feel ashamed that they didn't stand up to their attacker, or they feel complicit if they experience arousal, even though this is a normal physiological response.

Assumptions about what it means to be a man also make it more difficult to seek help, according to Daniel. "As men we're taught to always want sex, that it's something we should never say no to. We're taught that men stereotypically think about sex every five seconds, that this is at the forefront of our brains. We even refer to it as 'scoring,' as if it's a game, or something that we can win. To admit that this is something you didn't want is to almost strip yourself of the stereotypical ideal of manhood or masculinity."

Hope

Hope Brinn took nine AP classes, was a member of the math league and captain of the Science Olympiad team in high school. When she went to a party during her third week at Swarthmore College, it was the third one she'd ever been to.

The party was at a fraternity, one of just two fraternities at Swarthmore. At the party, a student from the fraternity approached Hope, put his arm around her, and steered her away from her friends. At first, she enjoyed the attention: "He was really nice, and he was sweet-talking me, and he handed me drink after drink, and you know, I was flattered; I was very, very flattered. Because I went to an all-girls Catholic high school; I wasn't really experienced at all in that way."

He suggested they go outside, and it was there that he pinned her against a wall, pulled off her clothes and sexually assaulted her. Hope tried to get free, but he wouldn't let her go. A friend finally came outside to look for Hope and helped her get away. The two ran away from her assailant, who chased them all the way back to the friend's dorm.

Hope initially brushed off the incident. "I thought, *He's just a weird drunk guy. It's not a big deal. Just a gross frat brother. I should have known.*" But the man wouldn't leave her alone: He kept approaching her at parties and pressing her to sleep with him; at other times he belittled and tried to humiliate her. Meanwhile he told his fraternity brothers that she was obsessively pursuing him. She later found out that the fraternity had a derisive nickname for her, and that they made fun of the frat brother for hooking up with her because they considered her so unattractive. At one point, someone broke into her room while she wasn't there, and the realization caused knots in her stomach.

Over time, Hope learned that the student had assaulted other women at Swarthmore, so she decided to report him. As a result, she was banned from the fraternity, and other friends turned on her. She didn't care about the ban but believes the gesture reflects an ethos that is responsible, at least in part, for Swarthmore's sexual assault problems. "It's this 'don't dick a bro' culture: You protect your brothers at all costs, in all circumstances, no matter what," she says. "It's this fake notion of brotherhood that I really, really can't wrap my mind around."

Despite the retaliation Hope received from fellow students and even some administrators at the college, she didn't stay silent. She joined other students in a Title IX complaint against the college, and reached out to survivors through a group called Swarthmore Assault Prevention and Survivor Advocacy. She and another student started a chalking campaign, scrawling messages about sexual assault in chalk around the campus.

There was a moment when Hope didn't speak up, and it haunts her. It happened before she reported her attack, before she acknowledged that she'd been sexually assaulted—even to herself. "I was coming back from my dorm and I saw my assailant walking into his room with a very, very intoxicated freshman who was not even really able to hold herself up," she recalls. "And I stood there, and he saw me, and I just stood outside of his door for a couple minutes and thought, *Should I call public safety? Should I call public safety?* And then I said to myself, *Well I don't know if he's going to assault her.* Now of course, I really did know. But I kept talking myself out of it. And I just—I still regret that to this day."

Natassja

The following survivor, Nastassja Schmiedt, identifies as gender queer, and goes by the gender neutral they/them pronoun.

Nastassja Schmiedt always wanted to go to an Ivy League school. "I could list the Ivys from the time that I was five years old," they recall. They were a top student at their high school in Miami, where they were one of few black students. Despite Nastassja's academic success, they were nervous when replies from colleges began rolling in. "I remember I got the acceptance letter from Dartmouth and I did a cartwheel," they said. "It was really, really, really exciting."

During their freshman year at Dartmouth, Nastassja came out as LGBTQ. Later that same year, Nastassja was sexually assaulted by a woman. The two were at a fraternity party, and the woman, who was a casual friend, kept giving Nastassja drinks. Later she walked Nastassja, who at that point was very drunk, back to their dorm and assaulted them.

Nastassja repeatedly told the woman that they did not want to have sex. The woman later told Nastassja that she had intentionally given Nastassja drinks in order to have sex.

Nastassja never reported the incident, and their reasons for not doing so reflect the complicated reality minority and LGBTQ assault survivors face. Nastassja was reluctant to report, in part, because their assailant was a gay woman of color—part of a group that Nastassja says is already marginalized on the Dartmouth campus. Nastassja also had little faith that Dartmouth administrators would pursue their case. The word around campus was that administrators typically did little to address assault reports; they assumed administrators would be even less likely to investigate an assault by a woman.

According to Nastassja, other LGBTQ survivors they've talked to show a similar ambivalence about their experience. "Their reaction is often, 'Is this something that is wrong? Or is this something that happens to people like me? Because if it's something that just happens to people like me, why would anyone care?'" Nastassja said.

While many campus assault survivors who have gone public have been white and heterosexual, research shows that in the general population, minorities and those who identify as LGBTQ experience higher rates of sexual violence than whites and heterosexuals do. While there has been little research on college campuses about this aspect of this issue, a 2015 campus survey at the University of Michigan found that LGBTQ and minority students there were shockingly twice as likely to experience sexual assault as their straight and non-minority peers were.

Nastassja went on personal leave from Dartmouth before the end of their sophomore year, after experiencing retaliation for their activism against sexual assault and other forms of campus violence. They co-founded Spring Up, a multimedia activist collective that advocates for campus safety and conducts antiviolence workshops on college campuses. Natassja recently co-authored a book about consent, desire, and intimacy titled *Millennial Sex Education: I've Never Done This Before.*

Jaclyn

Jaclyn Prado, who is half Hispanic, wanted to be the first in her family to graduate from college. Her childhood was rough: Her father, whom she adored, died when she was in seventh grade. After his death, her mother moved away from the small town in Iowa where Jaclyn was raised. Jaclyn stayed with her grandparents, then joined her mother in Missouri, then moved back to Iowa, where she bounced from one relative's home to another. At 17, she got an apartment on her own, supporting herself on Social Security checks and a weekend job as a waitress.

Despite the chaos and the couch-surfing, Jaclyn excelled in school. "I'm a nerd; I love school," she says. "Without having the family foundation at home, I used clubs and organizations to kind of build families. I was at school more than I was at home."

Jaclyn visited University of Denver (DU) during her senior year, and decided that that was where she wanted to go to college: "I walked on the campus. It was amazing," she recalls. "It's still amazing."

She received a scholarship to attend DU, and did well her first semester. Then, in March of that year, she went with friends to a fund-raiser at a Denver restaurant and bar. At some point during the party, a woman she didn't know offered her a drink. She believes the drink was drugged because she woke up some time later in a room she'd never seen before. A man she didn't know was on top of her. Her hands were cuffed behind her back. She lapsed in and out of consciousness as he repeatedly raped her. At one point, when she struggled and tried to push him off her, he grabbed her throat so hard she could barely breathe.

Jaclyn doesn't remember how she got free or how she made it back to her dorm. A friend found her at 3:00 a.m. in a state of shock. Her friend called the police, and Jaclyn was examined at the hospital. Photos were taken of bruises on her wrists, neck, and shoulders.

The incident was investigated by DU officials, and one official found "significant markings around plaintiff's neck, shoulder blades, and shoulders. [The offender] is unable to explain the presence of this level of bruising." But despite this evidence, the investigation concluded the male student "reasonably believed" Jaclyn was a willing participant. Her assailant wasn't expelled or sanctioned. Denver police also refused to file charges. Jaclyn finished the semester, then dropped out of school. She sued Denver University under Title IX.

Jaclyn's grandmother, Ronda Boeddeker, worries about how the assault has affected her: "She was so excited and so bubbly and so happy," she says. "She was going to win the world. And now she's just kind of tromped on."

Jaclyn admits that she has struggled since the attack. "Right now, honestly, if you were to ask me what's my action plan; what's my game plan? I don't have one. And my family doesn't have one for me either, of course. So I'm in Denver . . . . I'm in Denver where my rapist lives."

But she hasn't given up her dream of a college degree: "I want to be in school so bad, but I need this year to find a job, to get my feet back on the ground, to save money to go back. So I have my degree on hold. I can't look at the word 'dropout.' That's not me."

2

Sexual Assault in a Football Town

by Amy Herdy

PART 1

In June 2014, I stood at a podium looking out over the faces of Tallahassee's most prominent citizens, including law enforcement officials from three different agencies, and watched their welcoming smiles fade. Many of them held strong opinions against a young woman who had alleged being raped by the local football legend, and I was about to say some things they didn't want to hear.

As the keynote speaker at a benefit for Refuge House, an excellent local organization that provides services to survivors of domestic violence and sexual violence, I told the audience that their community needed to improve its response to campus sexual assault. I watched some people's expressions darken at what they no doubt considered rudeness by an outsider.

I had no regrets about what I'd said. I was speaking on behalf of many survivors of sexual assault who attended Florida State

University (FSU), the city's flagship school—all of whom had been doubted, demeaned, and abandoned by their school (and by local law enforcement, in some cases) when they reported their assaults.

I was also speaking directly to one survivor in particular—one whom I had never met, although I knew so much about her. And she wasn't even in the audience.

Many of those who keep up with the news know her name: Erica Kinsman. Erica is the Florida State University pre-med student who alleged she was sexually assaulted by Jameis Winston—an FSU athlete who would later quarterback the Seminoles football team to a national championship and win the Heisman Trophy, going on to be chosen as the number-one NFL draft pick by the Tampa Bay Buccaneers.

The case sparked widespread controversy over actions FSU and local law enforcement took to protect Winston, and it remains under investigation by the Department of Education's Office of Civil Rights. Erica filed suit against FSU, claiming the school violated her rights under Title IX, and in April 2015, she filed suit against Jameis Winston, alleging sexual battery, assault, false imprisonment, and intentional infliction of emotional distress arising out of forcible rape.

Erica, who received repeated threats after her name became public, initially refused all interview requests. She told her story on camera for the first time in the film *The Hunting Ground*. What follows is an account of our investigation—and one woman's search for justice in a football town.

"Someone Help Me"

In the spring of 2013, the two-time Academy Award-nominated documentary director Kirby Dick and producer Amy Ziering began working on a documentary about campus sexual assault—well before the issue had catapulted to the forefront of media attention. Shortly after they started the project, I began working for them as an investigative producer, performing research, lining up subjects to interview, and conducting interviews both on and off camera.

As soon as the Erica Kinsman story broke, our team began poring over the details of the case we learned from police reports and interviews:

On December 6, 2012, Erica, then an FSU freshman, accompanied friends to Potbelly's, a popular student bar. Erica was a serious student who didn't party a lot, and she didn't have much to drink that night. Shortly after midnight, she recounted how a strange man offered her a shot, and her mind became cloudy for the next several minutes. She would later recall finding herself outside the bar with three strange men pressuring her to get into a cab, and that, feeling afraid, she complied.

As the cab drove down the street, Erica would later say, she sat frozen with terror, fighting a rising belief that the men were going to take her to nearby woods, kill her, and dump her body. She would later say that at one point she could see a university administration building outside the vehicle's window, which gave her hope the three strange men were fellow students who wouldn't harm her, although one of them was fondling her in the cab, despite her attempts to push him away. Phone records show she used her cell phone to place two calls for help to her best friend, who did not answer. She said she considered asking the cab driver for help, but was afraid he would side with the men.

The cab then pulled up to an apartment building and she was taken to an apartment, where she later told police one of the men raped her in a bedroom while she begged him to stop, even as she lay motionless paralyzed with fear, focusing on the garnet-and-gold polka dot pattern on the sheets.

FSU sheets.

Erica told police the following: As she repeatedly said, "No," the man continued to rape her. At one point he tried to turn her over but was unable to do so. One of the other men then entered the room and said, "Dude, what are you doing? Stop. She's telling you to stop." Her attacker responded by lifting Erica by placing one hand under her legs and the other under her arms, and carrying her into the bathroom, where he laid her on the cold tile and locked the door. He then shoved her face into the floor, and climbed on top of her to rape her again. At this point, Erica began to fight, yelling, "Stop," trying to kick her attacker and twist away from him, but he held her down by pinning one arm and one leg, and raped her a second time.

Afterward, Erica recalled, she was so traumatized that she was unable to dress herself. The assailant dressed her, and then offered to take her home. Having no idea where she was or how she would get home, she agreed, and the man gave Erica a ride on the back of a scooter to an incorrect address she provided so he would not know where she lived. She climbed off the scooter and stood motionless in the street as she watched the man leave, and then, sobbing, she pulled out her cell phone, tweeting, "Someone help me." Two friends called her, and Erica told them both she had been raped. When she got to her room shortly after 2 a.m., one of her friends still wearing her pajamas, met her there, and after talking further, the two of them called 911 shortly after 3 a.m.

Both Tallahassee and FSU police responded and interviewed Erica, then Tallahassee police took her to Tallahassee Memorial Hospital, where she was examined and treated for vaginal trauma and other injuries. A rape examination was performed, and photos were taken of bruises starting to appear on her body.

At the time, Erica didn't know who her assailant was. Later she would say she was reporting the event only because she believed it was the right thing to do. When she returned to school after winter break, she recognized the man on the first day of a class in which they were both enrolled; Erica listened for his name during roll call and promptly provided it to the Tallahassee Police. His name was Jameis Winston; the name meant nothing to her. Erica didn't know at the time that Winston was the Florida State Seminoles' most highly recruited player who was taking a redshirt year and not playing as a freshman. At that point, he was an unknown.

A Credible Case

The more our team looked into Erica's story, the more certain we were it was true. A number of details underscored her credibility. For one thing, she reported the attack immediately. Her story was consistent, and those she spoke to supported her account. In addition, her reactions reflected distress, including the tweet, the 911 call, and the fact that she appeared extremely upset and crying in the initial hours after the assault. There was physical evidence of sexual trauma. Finally, the fact that, when she reported, she did not know who Winston was debunked accusations that his celebrity was a motive.

So we dug deeper, reaching out to Erica's friends and family members, witnesses, investigators, advocates involved in the case, and members of both the prosecution and defense teams.

We also interviewed a half-dozen FSU students who had reported sexual assaults to the school, and their stories shared patterns of discouragement and victim blaming.

Clearly, Erica's wasn't the only case that had been mishandled.

Anatomy of a Botched Police Investigation

After Erica identified Winston in January 2013, Scott Angulo, the detective handling the case, spoke to Erica's attorney, Patricia Carroll. When Carroll requested that a DNA swab be obtained from Winston, Detective Angulo refused. Carroll would later say that Angulo warned her it could cause the investigation to "go public." Carroll said that Angulo also told her that "Tallahassee was a big football town," and that if Erica pressed charges she would be harassed and probably forced to leave Tallahassee, adding, "Erica should 'think twice' before proceeding."

Although a medical examination of the victim revealed bruises and semen on her body—and the victim would identify Winston by name a month later—Tallahassee police didn't obtain a DNA sample from Winston until ordered to do so by the State Attorney's Office 10 months later. They also never interviewed him, and never attempted to obtain footage from Potbelly's, or a videotape of the encounter taken by his roommate. We requested Angulo's "jacket," or personnel file, and discovered that he did private security work for the Seminole Boosters, the primary financier of Florida State athletics—which raised questions about a possible conflict of interest. It also took Angulo two months to write his first report on the case, and then he suspended the investigation—without informing Erica.

Then on November 8, 2013, *Tampa Bay Times* reporter Matt Baker, acting on a tip, requested the police report on Winston.

Aware that the case was about to become public, FSU officials moved fast to create a chain of evidence to protect Winston. On November 13, Winston's lawyer, Tim Jansen, contacted Ronald Darby and Chris Casher, FSU football players who were in the apartment the morning of the alleged assault. Jansen arranged for the two to sign nearly identical statements in which they claimed they had seen a portion of the sexual encounter between Winston and Erica and it appeared consensual. The statements were signed before the state attorney's office received the case and one day before investigators attempted to interview the two about what they witnessed that night.

On December 4, 2013, nearly 11 months after Erica identified Winston, his DNA was finally tested and was matched with the DNA of the sperm from her rape kit. On December 5, 2013, State Attorney Willie Meggs announced the completion of the investigation and that no charges would be filed against Winston, citing a lack of independent evidence. Meggs stated, "As prosecutors, we only bring charges for cases where the evidence will result in a likely conviction at trial. In this case, the evidence does not show that."

A few weeks after that news conference, Meggs talked to us on camera about his frustrations with the lack of investigation. "Well, in this particular case, obviously we could've identified the suspect within five, six hours after the report," Meggs said. "The victim in the case had indicated that . . . a football player named Chris—there's only one—was who she had been talking to. So find him and go talk to him and you would've found out his roommate was Jameis Winston. So that could've been done the next morning. And, of course, it was not. Statements were not taken from them until 11 months later after we got involved in the case. The place where all of this started, a place called Potbelly's—a college hangout—has 30 cameras.

"Had we gone in December of '12 and looked at those cameras, we might have gained information that would be very valuable. So there was just a lot of things that needed to have been done that were not. And then by the time we got into it, all of that had been taped over and we got nothin' from Potbelly's. The cab driver that she left with . . . Tallahassee's not that big. We can find a cab driver. And we could've found him the next morning."

And when it came to contacting Winston for his version of events, Meggs said to Kirby, who was conducting the interview, he would have done it very differently.

"One of the things you do is obviously interview your victim and get your sexual assault kit done and then you have a statement at that point and go confront the defendant. And confront him on your terms, not on his.

"I would've found out that he was actually playing baseball, and they were in spring practice. I'd have probably walked up to him out on the practice field and said, 'Hey, come over here. I wanna talk to you a minute.' That's how I would've done it."

Not everyone considered the case to be weak. A forensic psychologist hired by Winston's FSU attorney, after talking to the attorney and reviewing the records, told me why he believed Winston was not held accountable: "The evidence, in my own opinion, was far more damning than some of the other cases that they [the state attorneys' office] tried to prosecute. I am convinced—and no one will ever admit to this—it was a function of it being Jameis Winston that happened."

Protecting a Star Athlete

FSU's investigation of the case was just as problematic.

On December 7, 2012, Erica had immediately reported her rape to Florida State University and Tallahassee police within hours of the assault. She was taken to a nearby hospital where a rape kit was administered and bruises were noted in her medical record. Yet FSU police did not report the assault to the FSU Title IX coordinator as required by federal guidelines.

On January 22, 2013, when head football coach Jimbo Fisher learned from Tallahassee police that Winston had been identified as the suspect in a violent sexual assault, Fisher also failed to report that information to the FSU Title IX coordinator as required by federal guidelines.

Instead, Fisher would later testify that on that same day, he and Monk Bonasorte, the second in command at the athletic department, would meet separately with Winston and his friends Casher and Darby, hire attorney Tim Jansen for Winston, and make the deliberate decision to not report the case further. FSU phone records would later reveal dozens of calls over the next three days made among Fisher, Bonasorte, Tallahassee police, FSU police, and several FSU officials.

For the next 18 months, FSU did almost nothing to investigate this rape report, even though the FSU school policy and the Department of Education presume that any accusation of sexual assault will be investigated and resolved within 60 days.

That was not the only case against Winston that would be blocked. We discovered that a second young woman was receiving counseling from an FSU rape victim advocate after a traumatizing sexual encounter with Winston that she had reported to a FSU housing official. That housing official in turn told FSU's dean of students, Jeanine Ward-Roof, who then began a Title IX investigation. Meanwhile, the second young woman began counseling at the victim's advocate's office.

Ashton then informed Erica's FSU victim advocate of the second sexual assault case, and that advocate asked Erica if she wanted her case to be a part of that investigation. When asked,

Erica responded that if the other woman was moving forward with her case, then she would like to do so as well.

When FSU Police Chief David Perry found out that Erica was told of the second victim, he strenuously objected. On November 12, 2013, despite being on notice that two women had reported being raped by Winston, Dean of Students Jeanine Ward-Roof, who supervised Code of Conduct proceedings at FSU, emailed Police Chief Perry and others at FSU reassuring them that no disciplinary proceedings against Winston were going to take place.

Ward-Roof copied her boss, Vice President Mary Coburn, on the email, which said, "It is not likely we would tell a victim that the accused was involved with another case unless we were moving forward with a conduct case . . . that is not the fact . . . ."

On November 14, 2013, feeling abandoned and alone, Erica dropped out of school, fearing for her safety because of retaliation over social media from FSU students and fans.

Meanwhile, Winston's stardom continued to rise, and on December 14, 2013, he was named winner of the 2013 Heisman Trophy. The following month, on January 6, 2014, FSU's football team won the BCS National Championship.

With the National Championship under their belt, on January 23, 2014, FSU finally called Winston in for an interview regarding the accusation—more than a year after FSU officials were made aware that Winston was accused of rape. It would prove futile, as Winston refused to answer any questions. After the interview, FSU sent a letter to Winston stating they were not going to investigate the case. The reason? Winston had refused to talk to them.

Yet Erica was still asking for an investigation. So in the spring of 2014, FSU, in violation of the victim advocate privilege, gave a copy of her privileged victim advocate file to its outside legal counsel.

Finally, beginning December 2, 2014, nearly two years after Erica reported being raped, FSU held a two-day hearing about the accusation. On December 21, the hearing officer, Justice Major B. Harding—who was paid $43,321.70 by FSU—found Winston not responsible, despite the fact he refused to answer nearly every question put to him, while Kinsman answered all 156 questions asked of her. Winston initially refused to answer any questions at all, but finally assented to vaguely answering these three:

HARDING: I would like to know in what manner, verbally or physically, that she gave consent.
WINSTON: Both, Your Honor, verbally and physically.
HARDING: And what did she say and what did she do?
WINSTON: Moaning is mostly physical. Well, moaning is physically. And verbally at that time, Your Honor.
HARDING: Well, that was during the sexual encounter?
WINSTON: Yes, Your Honor.
HARDING: Okay. All right. Thank you.

Harding found Winston not responsible for violating FSU's student conduct code (i.e., for sexual assault) despite the fact that the conduct code requires verbal consent of sexual encounters. The conduct code states in part: "Consent is not freely given if no clear verbal consent is given." *Merriam Webster* defines verbal as "relating to or consisting of words." Moaning is by definition not "verbal" and is certainly not "clear verbal consent." The two-day hearing produced absolutely no evidence that Winston received the required consent, but that didn't stop FSU from absolving their star quarterback.

On January 7, 2015, six days after his final football game of the season, Winston withdrew from FSU and made himself eligible for the 2015 NFL Football Draft. On April 30, he became the top draft pick, selected by the Tampa Bay Buccaneers.

Speaking Up, Speaking Out

It was the end of May 2014, and Kirby and Amy needed to wrap up shooting the major segments for the film. We had everything we needed to present the compelling FSU case in *The Hunting Ground* except the most important element: an interview with Erica Kinsman. Our repeated interview requests to her legal team always garnered the same answer: no.

There was no way we could include a segment on FSU without that critical interview, so Kirby and Amy began making plans to include a different story. But I wasn't giving up.

The executive director of Refuge House had asked me to be the keynote speaker in January for an upcoming event planned in April, and after it was postponed twice, it was set for the exact week in June my husband and I were moving from Colorado to a farm on San Juan Island in Washington state, a multi-trip endeavor involving dogs, cats, and horses, including a pregnant mare. A friend suggested I simplify my life and cancel on Refuge House, and I briefly considered it, but I had given my word. So I packed a small suitcase of work clothes among the mountains of moving boxes, and a few days later, flew across the country to Tallahassee to present my keynote speech at the event.

I spent hours working on my presentation. I'd spoken to so many FSU survivors, and I was passionate and angry on their behalf. I poured my heart into that talk; I figured if we couldn't feature Erica's case in the film, the public should at least know what we had learned. I also clung to the hope that somehow, Erica would hear about the talk, understand that we believed her, and agree to do the interview. It seemed the longest of shots.

In my speech, I didn't bother to conceal my anger. I expressed contempt for the Tallahassee investigator who had dismissed Erica's outcry of "Someone help me" as a new student asking for directions. I pointed out that FSU took more than a year and a half to schedule a hearing in her case, although the Department of Education recommends a time frame of 60 days, and I described how FSU treated her—and others who came forward to report assaults—with distrust and disdain.

Finally, I made the statement that caused heated mutters around the room: "I have thoroughly researched this case—including talking to witnesses who investigators did not—and I firmly believe that Jameis Winston raped that young woman."

After my speech, I was engaged in a deep conversation with a reporter when I felt a tap on my shoulder. I turned and recognized Erica's aunt. "Remember me?" she said, and then gestured to a woman standing next to her. "Someone wants to meet you." I found myself face to face with Erica Kinsman's mother, Teresa Kinsman, who stared at me with tears in her eyes.

In that moment I was struck by the magnitude of the pain this woman had endured as she watched her daughter suffer throughout this horrific ordeal. As a mother myself, my heart went out to her. My own eyes filled with tears and I said the first thing that came to mind: "Can I hug you?"

Later, we retreated to a quiet room away from the crowd, and Teresa Kinsman told me how much my talk had meant to her.

"I wish that other people knew what you did," she said, "so they would know the truth."

I took a deep breath. "There is a way for the truth to be known," I told her. "If Erica is in the film."

And that's exactly what happened. Erica Kinsman agreed to speak publicly for the first time in the film, *The Hunting Ground*.

During the interview, Erica was calm and extraordinarily composed. Here was a young woman who had unwittingly taken on the powerful institution of college sports—which was far more interested in making her go away than in stopping the clock to find out what actually happened. She'd endured what now amounted to years of hateful messages from Winston's supporters; both her sorority and her family had also been threatened. She had dropped out of FSU, while her alleged assailant had gone on to a promising career in the NFL.

Still, she remained stoic until Amy asked her one simple question: "Is it hard for you to believe that this all has happened?"

At that moment, you could see the depth of pain in Erica's eyes as they filled with tears. "I just want to know, why me?" she replied, her voice breaking. "It doesn't really make sense."

When I finally met Erica in person, I was struck, as I always am when I talk to campus assault survivors, by how young she was. And yet she had the courage to speak out, even when FSU administrators, law enforcement officials, and fans did everything they could to silence her. As she says in the film, "I know that was the right thing to do, to come forward. But investigator Angulo was right when he said that I would be driven out of Tallahassee."

PART 2

A Failed Attempt to Silence the Truth

Kirby and Amy led the way for our team to bring *The Hunting Ground* to the 2015 Sundance Film Festival, working 16-hour days for months before the January premiere. It reflected two years' worth of interviewing survivors, perpetrators, advocates, faculty, administrators, and law enforcement. We had reviewed thousands of pages of records and reports.

In the most comprehensive portrayal of this topic ever produced, the film gave voice to dozens of young women and men who courageously spoke on camera about their sexual assault and how their college or university responded. We spent hundreds of hours going over their cases and paperwork, verifying details and asking for records, emails, and contacts for corroboration. We spent dozens of hours on a rigorous fact-checking process with CNN news executives and their legal team. The film was solid and we knew it.

A packed audience attended the documentary's premiere, and we sat among them, observing reactions on people's faces as they watched the film. For the first time ever, an audience heard Erica Kinsman, who had identified Florida State University quarterback Jameis Winston as her rapist, speak publicly. In her straightforward manner, Erica shared her experience of how the school and the local police department botched the investigation, taking an enormous toll on her and her family. Many watching in the audience reacted to her story with indignant anger. Some quietly cried.

The film was released theatrically five weeks later, to rave reviews. Almost immediately, the backlash began.

In March 2015, FSU President John Thrasher released a statement condemning the film, claiming it was a "distorted presentation" and "erroneous," although he was unable to list one fact in the film that was incorrect. He further claimed that "the first time the University was contacted by the filmmakers was December 18," when in fact we made our first record request about the case nearly a year earlier.

Thrasher went on to say, "The University went to extraordinary lengths to support Ms. Kinsman and to initiate an impartial, independent Title IX investigation of her allegations against Mr. Winston." We had thousands of pages of documentation that proved that this was false; rather than undertaking a legally required investigation, they had engaged in a cover-up.

We were not surprised by Thrasher's aggressive reaction. In fact, as we showed repeatedly in our film, FSU was reacting in the same way most colleges and universities had historically reacted to charges of mishandling reports of sexual assault: by denying they have a problem and attacking the media.

However, even as FSU attacked *The Hunting Ground*, other colleges and universities were screening the film on their campuses and embracing it as a valuable tool to raise awareness. Ultimately, more than a thousand screenings have been held at campuses and community centers around the country, each screening beginning the valuable and often-difficult discussion about how to create safer campuses and support survivors.

Meanwhile, President Thrasher and FSU continued to try to bury the incident, paying the crisis communications firm G.F. Bunting+Co hundreds of thousands of dollars to try to prevent the truth from getting out. Shortly after Erica's case became public, representatives from Bunting began calling reporters from national news organizations assigned to the story, trying to discourage them from covering the case, misleading them with slanted information, and interfering with their attempts to schedule interviews with administrators.

In March 2015, we invited President Thrasher to attend a screening of the film followed by a panel discussion, and to engage in an open and productive discussion about sexual assault on college campuses. He declined. We went ahead with the screening anyway, held at a local theater. In the Q&A that followed, as sexual assault advocates and survivors began to speak, it became apparent how vilified Erica Kinsman had been for speaking out against the school's star quarterback. One audience member stood up and said that this was the first time she had heard Erica's name mentioned in a positive context since the story became public a year and a half earlier.

In the summer of 2015, a CNN executive announced in a media interview that *The Hunting Ground* was scheduled to air on CNN for the fall. Behind the scenes, Bunting sent a long, strongly worded email to CNN executives, falsely claiming that the film was flawed, and that we had been reckless and inaccurate. We once again gave CNN our backup documentation and evidence, which clearly refuted every claim that Bunting had made.

A few weeks later, Bunting sent CNN two emails I had written to Erica Kinsman's aunt and first attorney, Patricia Carroll. FSU had obtained the emails after serving a subpoena on Carroll (they served subpoenas on the filmmaking team, as well, but our First Amendment attorneys successfully fought them). In the first email, sent in November 2013, I introduced myself to Carroll and asked for an interview with Kinsman, her niece, telling her that the film team were advocates and that the interview would not include "insensitive questions or the need to get the perpetrator's side." In the second email, I told Carroll that the film team was planning to do an "ambush" interview should the man Kinsman had identified as her assailant, football star Jameis Winston, turn down our interview request.

Reading the two isolated emails gave an outsider no sense of their context or background. Jameis Winston was a high-profile athlete named in two separate sexual assaults that we knew of at the time. He had not only refused to speak to any media, but had also dodged six other formal requests by law enforcement and education officials to answer questions regarding the rape allegations against him. The term "ambush interview" refers to a tactic often used by journalists and media outlets to get a response from public figures who refuse repeated interview requests. In the end, we did not use this tactic. We made multiple attempts to interview Winston, reaching out to him and to his attorney, and offering to fly him to Los Angeles or meet him in Florida. Neither he nor his attorney responded.

I remember talking to Patricia Carroll about the interview before sending her that email. She is a dedicated woman who deeply loves her niece, and who herself was traumatized by what Kinsman had endured. Carroll had made it clear to me that she was very protective and afraid her niece would be further traumatized by our interview process; she feared that through our questions, we would subject Kinsman to yet another attack by her perpetrator. My goal was to reassure her and to get a first meeting. Anyone who has worked with me in the past, whether at the *St. Petersburg Times*, *The Denver Post*, or KUSA-TV in Denver, or as a journalism instructor for clients that have included the U.S. State Department, knows that I stress fairness, both in my work and in my teaching. I understood the intent of the email but the wording of it remains something I regret.

By the fall of 2015, when it became apparent that Bunting's ploy did not work, FSU took another approach. Thrasher released an open letter to the press on November 16, 2015, denouncing both the film and CNN, which was promoting the November 22 broadcast debut. The letter, which claimed that FSU was a "model" for other schools regarding sexual assault, read in part: "I want to make one thing clear: FSU does not tolerate rape. Period."

Within days of Thrasher's claim, the *New York Times* exposed the falseness of Thrasher's statement, reporting how FSU's former victim advocate director had testified that 40 football players had been accused of either sexual assault or intimate partner violence and only one found responsible. Later, *USA Today* followed with a story that revealed that during 2014 alone, the FSU victim advocate's office interacted with 828 new students who had reported being victims of sexual battery, sexual misconduct, and sexual assault.

Then on November 20, Jameis Winston's attorneys sent a letter to Jeff Zucker, president of CNN Worldwide, threatening to sue the network if it went forward with the broadcast. Undeterred, CNN aired the film on the 22nd, garnering enthusiastic audiences and strong accolades. It aired again in December, causing an outpouring of support and a 20-percent increase in calls to a national rape crisis center.

The next month, nearly a year to the day after the film's debut at Sundance, FSU announced it was settling Erica's lawsuit against the school over how it had mishandled her Title IX case. The landmark settlement paid $950,000 to Erica and ensured that FSU would institute reforms in the way it handles sexual assault cases over a five-year period. The settlement, viewed as a victory for survivors everywhere, was a testament not only to Erica's courage but also to how the voice of a single survivor can make a difference. According to Baine Kerr, one of Erica's attorneys, "FSU instituted prevention, training, and awareness programs that would never have been introduced without this case."

Unfortunately, Thrasher, rather than use the settlement as an opportunity to bring the FSU community together to address the problem of sexual assault on its campus, continued to respond aggressively. In a statement called "disingenuous and meanspirited" by the *New York Times*, Thrasher claimed the school would have won the lawsuit had it continued, and that they settled only in order to be "financially responsible." The truth was that their chief of police and former dean of students, both of whom had supported the FSU party line in the case, were scheduled to be deposed within weeks, and FSU did not want that information made public. Of even more concern to FSU, the person at the very center of the cover-up, Jameis Winston, was also scheduled to be deposed, and his revelations (assuming he answered questions and told the truth) could have been damaging front-page news for the university.

The *New York Times* piece read: "Everything Florida State has done since the beginning of the Winston affair—from looking the other way until a national championship was in hand, to using the settlement to heap scorn on the accuser's lawsuit—has sent one message to its student body: Athletic achievement matters more than the students' safety . . . . If Thrasher had been honest, that's what he would have said in his statement."

Thrasher's refusal to take responsibility or provide leadership infuriated readers: "My wife and I are both FSU graduates, we loved our time there," one reader wrote in the comment section following the *New York Times* piece. "Now when we get calls from the alumni office asking for donations we respond that we cannot, in good conscience, give to a misogynist school that coddles rapists and denigrates their victims."

Another reader wrote, "I was a scholarship athlete at FSU forty-five years ago, and the only thing that is different is that at least this time there are some (admittedly inadequate) consequences to the school—but of course, not the perpetrator."

Others made it clear they believed FSU fostered a dangerous environment: "No way can I, in good conscience, send daughters whom I love more than life itself to a place harboring such an attitude," one reader wrote.

"Until schools like FSU put their students' safety first, no way would I consider putting my child there," said another.

The ripple effect from Erica's case will no doubt continue for years to come, and more details concerning the extent of FSU's cover-up will likely be revealed. Meanwhile, one thing remains certain: The extraordinary and heroic efforts of Erica to hold FSU accountable will have a positive impact on thousands of lives.

For more than twenty years, Amy Herdy has specialized in investigative and trauma journalism. A 2003 investigative series Herdy coauthored at the Denver Post, *"Betrayal in the Ranks," spurred Congressional reforms. Herdy has taught workshops on investigative reporting and trauma journalism for the U.S. State Department in Lahore, Karachi, and Islamabad, Pakistan. Her awards include an Emmy; Society of Professional Journalists awards; a Radio, Television News Directors Association award; an Associated Press award; two American Society of Newspaper Editors awards and a Military Reporters & Editors award. Herdy is the author of an award-winning memoir,* Diary of a Predator, *about covering the case of serial rapist Brent Brents. She was the investigative producer for* The Hunting Ground *film, and is now a producer for Chain Camera Pictures.*

3

The Woman Who Stood Up to Harvard Law

by Kirby Dick and Amy Ziering

Shortly after we started investigating sexual assault on college campuses, we began hearing about problems at Harvard. We were put in touch with more than a half-dozen students who had been assaulted there, but none of them wanted to go on camera to talk about it. Some felt that they had worked so hard to get to Harvard, and that the school was such an important step toward their career, that they didn't want to do anything that might trigger institutional backlash. Then we met Kamilah Willingham, a recent graduate of Harvard Law, who had been assaulted while there and was willing to speak on the record.

We were introduced to Kamilah by Colby Bruno, an attorney with the Boston-based Victim Rights Law Center, a nonprofit law center devoted solely to giving pro bono legal aid to victims of rape and sexual assault. Since the Center became a nonprofit in 2003, it has served hundreds of victims who've been sexually assaulted in college, including women like Kamilah who needed help navigating her school's Title IX process.

Kamilah is intelligent and poised, with a quiet but powerful demeanor and a strong sense of integrity and justice, all reminiscent of a young Anita Hill. And just as in Hill's case, the man Kamilah named as her perpetrator responded not only with denial but with a counter attack that included portraying Kamilah as a spurned woman. And just as Hill was found to be credible in her story of being sexually harassed by Clarence Thomas, so, too, was Kamilah found credible by three different bodies within Harvard Law—until a group of professors took it upon themselves to overturn the findings of her case, allow her perpetrator to return to Harvard, and then retaliate against her when she spoke out about her experience.

Unconscious and Incapable of Consent

By her third year at Harvard Law, Kamilah was garnering praise from her professors for her academic achievements and strong sense of social justice. Yet in the early morning hours of January 15, 2011, the foundation of Kamilah's world at Harvard would crumble.

The evening began with Kamilah getting together with a friend (identified as "AB" to protect her privacy), and Brandon Winston, a Harvard Law student whom she considered to be a trusted male friend. They spent the next six hours drinking, and then Kamilah and AB fell asleep fully clothed at Kamilah's apartment. Kamilah recounts awakening to find Winston on top of her attempting to have sex, and then seeing him fondle AB's naked breast and admitting to Kamilah that he had disrobed her. The following day, Kamilah contacted the Harvard Office of Sexual Assault Prevention

& Response for help. Then, on January 18, 2011, Kamilah and AB together reported their assaults to the Cambridge Police as well. In April, Kamilah, concerned for the safety of other students, filed a complaint with the Harvard Law School. The school appointed an independent fact finder (an attorney not employed by the school) to undertake a three-month investigation that included lengthy interviews of Kamilah, AB, and Winston.

On August 10, 2011, the fact finder released a report that found Kamilah's account of the events "was credible" while Winston's account was found to be "was not credible," and that neither Kamilah nor AB had consented to Winston to engaging in sexual conduct with them. The fact finder also found that:

- Winston's "actions in undressing AB, touching her body, rubbing her crotch, and inserting his finger in AB's vagina, when she was incapacitated by alcohol intoxication, were abusive and unreasonably invasive."
- Winston did not "offer a reasonable explanation for his statement that he put 'a finger briefly in the v at most'."
- Winston "changed his account at least two times."

On September 19, 2011, the Harvard Law Administrative Board conducted a daylong hearing on Kamilah's complaint against Winston. After reviewing all of the evidence, the Board found that:

- Winston "had initiated sexual conduct with the complainant [Willingham] while she was asleep or unconscious, and not capable of consenting."
- Winston "had initiated sexual contact with the friend while she was incapable of consenting."

As a result, on September 21, 2011, the Board recommended the sanction of dismission (expulsion with option to apply for readmission) for Winston. Winston initiated an appeal, which was heard by the appeal hearing officer. After reviewing the case, the hearing officer upheld the Administrative Board's findings. And then the Harvard Law faculty stepped in.

A Secretive and Flawed Process Lets a Perpetrator Back On Campus

The Harvard Law faculty reviewed the case, and even though they had not heard direct testimony from any of the parties involved, they overturned the findings and recommendations of Harvard Law's investigative fact finder, Administrative Board, and appeal hearing officer, and allowed Winston to return to campus.

Kamilah was not notified of the faculty process or its decision until months after Winston was notified (a violation of Title IX guidelines), and after he was allowed to return to campus, where Kamilah had just begun a post-graduate teaching fellowship. Harvard Law refused to inform Kamilah who was present at the Harvard Law faculty vote or what the vote count was, or what the specific reason was for overturning the findings, other than to vaguely say that the "findings were not supported by substantial evidence." When Kamilah requested a written or digital copy of the decision, the dean of Harvard Law refused to provide her with one.

Kamilah then filed a complaint against Harvard Law under Title IX with the U.S. Department of Education's Office of Civil Rights (OCR), which began to investigate the school. They found that the Harvard Law adjudication process, especially the faculty review process, was flawed and in violation of guidelines of Title IX law. In particular, the Department found that Harvard Law's policies unfairly favored perpetrators.

In the December 2014 settlement agreement that followed between the Department of Education and Harvard Law, Harvard Law was required to reform its adjudication processes. The agreement detailed more than two-dozen specific requirements addressing issues of training, policy awareness, and procedures that adhere to Title IX. In its press release about the settlement, the Department chose to highlight one case that was particularly egregious. Although names were not provided, every indication is that the case was Kamilah's—a clear rebuke of Harvard Law's process and decision.

In the settlement agreement, OCR appeared to address the faculty directly when it said, "[N]o school or unit-based policy, procedure or process can reverse or alter a factual finding, remedy, or other decision made through the University's Title IX Policy and Procedures." To ensure Harvard Law followed its directives, the agreement also stipulated that OCR would monitor Harvard Law for a three-year period. It is clear that if the school had followed Title IX guidelines, the sanction against Winston would not have been overturned.

Meanwhile, the County of Middlesex had been moving forward with a criminal investigation. In September 2012, prosecutors from the Middlesex District Attorney's Office presented charges to a Middlesex Superior Court grand jury against Winston for the assault of Kamilah and her friend. The grand jury indicted Winston on two felony counts of indecent assault and battery (the equivalent of felony sexual assault) against Kamilah's friend. In March 2015, a jury convicted Winston of misdemeanor nonsexual assault for touching the breast of an incapacitated woman.

The victim advocate who worked with the prosecutor explained to Kamilah and her friend that the conviction was a victory, since juries rarely convict for anything at all in sexual assault cases, especially in cases where the assailant is a friend.

The statistics are not in the favor of victims regarding sexual assault: The U.S. Department of Justice estimates that only 32 percent of victims report their sexual assault, and that only three out of every 100 rapists will serve any prison time. Since only an exceedingly small percentage of sexual assault cases are ever prosecuted and even fewer result in any kind of conviction, this case was, in its own small way, a win for survivors everywhere.

A Shameful Media Attack

Three months later, Emily Yoffe, a columnist with a history of denying the truth about the prevalence of sexual assault and blaming sexual assault survivors, published a column in *Slate* that falsely claimed Kamilah's account in *The Hunting Ground* was flawed. True to form, Yoffe's piece smeared Kamilah. She presented the perpetrator's one-sided version of events through his defense attorney, without doing even the most basic fact-checking. She failed to talk with the prosecutor or Kamilah, and ignored thousands of pages of documentation on the case, resulting in a piece that contained dozens of factul errors and misrepresentations.

She stated Kamilah waited three months after the assault to report; in fact, Kamilah reported within forty-eight hours. Yoffe also falsely claimed that neither Harvard nor the local prosecutor "found evidence to substantiate Willingham's claims in *The Hunting Ground*." The truth is that Harvard Law's fact finder, Administrative Board, and appeal hearing officer, as well as Middlesex County's prosecutor, and Middlesex County's grand jury, all found conclusive evidence to support her claims. In her rush to defend Harvard Law, Yoffe failed to even mention that the same body of professors who overturned the findings in Kamilah's case did so using a flawed process that was found by the Department of Education to be in violation of Title IX law.

In spite of the vehemence of Yoffe's attack, she failed to disprove anything in Kamilah's account of the events or in the film's description of them. Her piece was so flawed that the online publication *Jezebel* ran a lengthy refutation of it, and *Slate* subsequently acknowledged multiple errors.

Protecting Reputation Rather Than Students

Shortly before the film's November 2015 broadcast debut on CNN, nineteen Harvard Law professors, stung by the film's exposure of their involvement in a flawed process, issued a public statement slamming the film's portrayal of Kamilah's story. They defended their decision to allow Winston to return to school, failing to mention that the entities that actually spoke directly to the witnesses—the Administrative Board and appeal hearing officer—recommended his dimission. And, like Yoffe, they failed to mention that the process they participated in was a direct violation of the U.S. Department of Education guidelines on Title IX law.

As with Yoffe's article, their piece was full of factual errors and misleading statements. The professors stated that, "[T]here was never any evidence that [the accused] used force," even though nowhere in the film is the use of force against Kamilah or her friend stated or even suggested. This claim was not only inaccurate, it indicated these professors harbored antiquated perceptions of rape, such as the notion that for a rape to take place, force must be used.

In fact, force is not involved in most sexual assaults, especially those on campuses. According to one study, more than 50 percent of sexual assaults happen while the victim is incapacitated. By emphasizing force, these professors were in essence saying that unless force is involved, it is less likely that a sexual assault occurred, or if it did, it is not something that should not be taken as seriously as one involving force.

Another of the professors' accusations was to question the "general sexual assault phenomenon" the film portrays. It's deeply troubling that these Harvard Law professors, without any expertise or evidence to support their claim, engaged in challenging decades of well-founded studies that show that one in five women will be sexually assaulted in college.

Additionally, the professors argued that because Winston had not been found guilty of sexual assault in the criminal process, they were therefore vindicated for not finding him responsible in the Harvard Law process. This argument is particularly specious: The criminal and Harvard Law (civil) processes require two different standards of proof, a fact the professors deliberately failed to note. The criminal standard "beyond a reasonable doubt" is much higher than the civil standard, which is why OJ Simpson could be found not guilty in criminal court but would later go on to lose the civil lawsuit. The fact that law professors at the most esteemed law school in the country would conflate the two processes and intentionally mislead the public is reprehensible, and shows the lengths they are willing to go to defend their involvement in a flawed process.

Even more troubling, the professors failed to mention the epidemic of sexual assault at their institution, and exhibited no concern whatsoever for survivors. The real injustice at the heart of this issue is that these Harvard Law professors have been completely silent regarding the thousands of assaults that have happened on their campus for decades—assaults that have not been properly investigated or adjudicated. Not once in their statement did they acknowledge that nearly 30 percent of women are sexually assaulted while at Harvard, nor did they express any concern for these victims. Their silence contributes to the ongoing problem of sexual assault at Harvard and Harvard Law.

A Chilling Message, and a Monetary Motivation

Many members of the Harvard community let us know that the critical nineteen Harvard Law professors were the minority. Harvard Law faculty member Diane Rosenfeld stated: "I fully support *The Hunting Ground* film, which is all about ending the silence of survivors. The signatories of the press release represent only a minority of the HLS faculty."

Members of The Harassment/Assault Legal Team (HALT), a law student–run organization that advocates for victims of campus sexual harassment and assault, came out in strong support of the film as well, releasing the following statement:

> The creators of *The Hunting Ground* gave survivors a chance to tell their story, which is a different task from courtroom advocacy, though no less noble. To some of our professors, it seems, sharing one's story in a documentary, speaking outside of the legal arena, causes discomfort. But they don't want her to tell her story publicly; at least not without all the facts they think need to be included, and certainly not after they've decided she was lying. Targeting the forum in which a survivor speaks is another way of silencing the survivor.

The nineteen members of Harvard Law's faculty would do well to learn from those students. Rather than acknowledging their involvement in Harvard Law's unfair process, these faculty members instead tried to publicly discredit Kamilah, even going so far as to team up with the assailant's defense attorney to build a biased website against her.

We agree with law professors and attorneys around the country who have publicly stated that the professors' actions were an embarrassment to individuals of their stature and to Harvard Law, and that it was wrong for these professors who had adjudicated this case to later side with one of their former students against another in this way. We also believe these aggressive actions send a very chilling message to all current and future students at Harvard and Harvard Law: If you report a sexual assault, your professors may come after you publicly. What student would report a sexual assault if they know this might happen? Very few—and when fewer assaults are reported, rapists are free to continue to assault, and the school becomes a more dangerous place.

For several weeks after the film aired on CNN, Harvard faculty members continued their misinformation campaign, issuing statements and social media messages that discredited Kamilah and the film.

Why would these nineteen professors, without the facts on their side, go after the film and their former student in such a public way? Other schools had been rightfully criticized, both in the film and by the media, and with the exception of FSU, none had responded so aggressively.

One explanation was suggested very early in the filmmaking process. Director Kirby Dick, when speaking with a national expert on college sexual assault, was told, "The Ivy League schools are the worst, because they are the most arrogant, and they think no one can tell them what to do." (Fortunately, a number of the nation's other elite schools, including Yale, Amherst, Wesleyan, and UCLA, among others, have shifted their approach, beginning to focus more on reforming their polices than protecting their reputations.)

Another reason, which has been articulated by faculty at several law schools including Harvard Law, was that many of these nineteen professors had publicly disagreed with the Office of Civil Rights' interpretation of Title IX law, taking the position that "the faculty believes they know better than OCR." After Kamilah filed an OCR complaint, and OCR responded by issuing a public rebuke of the Harvard Law faculty process, these nineteen professors, bitterly stung by both OCR's critique and *The Hunting Ground's* examination of their errors, decided to discredit Kamilah and the film as a way of striking back against OCR.

There is a third factor that may be at play as well, one that not surprisingly involves money. The film had been publicly available for nearly ten months before people associated with Harvard Law began attacking Willingham's account of her assault. These attacks began on November 11—just eight days after Harvard launched a $305 million fund-raising campaign. Harvard Law appears to be doing what *The Hunting Ground* shows universities have done for the past fifty years: discrediting survivors to protect their own reputations and funding sources, all at the expense of their students' safety and well-being.

Through it all, Kamilah continues to be the embodiment of courage. She refuses to back down, even after some of her former professors came after her. She came forward to report the assault for the same reason most survivors do: to prevent their assailant from doing it again. Kamilah knows this isn't just about her or her assailant; this is about justice and safety for millions of others. And she says she's willing to continue that fight, no matter how difficult and painful it might be. This country is becoming a better place because of Kamilah and the other women and men around the country who are standing up to their institutions and demanding they protect their students.

4

Fraternities and Sexual Assault

What is it about Greek culture that makes sexual assault so common? Why don't college and fraternity administrators do more to stop these crimes? To learn more about the link between fraternities and sexual assault, Kirby Dick and Amy Ziering turned to two experts: writer Caitlin Flanagan and attorney Doug Fierberg, as well as three University of California, Berkeley students who know the fraternity scene first-hand.

Caitlin Flanagan, a contributing writer for *The Atlantic,* spent a year researching the history and culture of U.S. fraternities for her groundbreaking 2015 article "The Dark Power of Fraternities." The article examines how the fraternity system routinely shifts the blame (and the cost) of fraternity assaults and accidents onto students and their families. It also exposes the powerful interests that protect Greek life, and the complicated relationships between fraternities and the universities that host them.

Douglas Fierberg was the first attorney in the country to exclusively represent victims of school violence. He represented victims of the shooting at Virginia Tech and families of those killed during a campus massacre in Alabama. He has also represented victims of hazing and sexual assault—including gang rape—at fraternities around the country. Flanagan praises Fierberg's legal expertise in her *Atlantic* article, saying "He is the man I would run to as though my hair were on fire if I ever found myself in a legal battle with a fraternity, and so should you."

Dick and Ziering interviewed Flanagan and Fierberg for *The Hunting Ground*, and Ziering spoke at length with the three young women from Berkeley. The following are excerpts from those conversations.

Interview with Caitlin Flanagan on Greek Culture

Kirby Dick: What first got you interested in researching fraternities?

Caitlin Flanagan: Well, I went to the University of Virginia [for college]. I went to fraternity parties and I thought this was the center of the world—these big, beautiful mansions with these columns out front and music pouring out. I have this really strong memory of watching a young guy lean this girl back on a front balcony in front of a fan light. She had this long hair and he was kissing her and I just thought this was the most romantic thing I've ever seen.

And then people began quietly taking me aside and telling me I had to be very careful around the fraternities. We didn't really have the language that people have today—even the language of date rape was very new—but I started to understand they were talking about sexual assault and rape.

My boyfriend was in a fraternity. I knew a lot of great guys who were in fraternities. I liked him, but it didn't really work out. When we were breaking up we were at a restaurant and he grabbed my hand across the table and said, "Cait, you have to promise me something." And I said, "What?" And he said, "Promise me you'll never go upstairs alone in a fraternity house."

And I said, "Yeah, yeah, yeah, I get it." And he said, "No, listen to me. You have to promise that you'll never do that." I later learned that the drugging and raping of young women in the fraternity houses in the early 1980s was a pretty widespread practice.

When I began writing my *Atlantic* article I thought that would have changed. You know, because everything for young women at the University of Virginia—at *all* colleges and universities—has changed so much for the better. The subjects they study, the aspirations they have for themselves, the leadership roles they have on campus, the athletics—everything's changed. But it hasn't. When it comes to fraternities, the only thing women have to protect themselves are people telling them quietly and secretly and grabbing their hand and whispering. It hasn't changed a bit.

And there's a reason why so many freshman women end up being the ones raped at fraternities. It takes a while to meet enough people to get information about what's happening because the administration of the university won't tell these young women. They are in league with the fraternities and they're not in league with the young women.

KD: What's happening with fraternities and sexual assault?
CF: The American fraternity industry is a vast industry and it spans thousands of American colleges, from the most elite private Ivy League institutions to small regional colleges. It's an incredibly well-funded network. They have tremendous liability in terms of personal injury. We all know about prevalence of inflicted trauma from hazing. But it's a matter of public record that the second-most-common type of insurance claim against the fraternity industry is for rape.

I think it's a national scandal. I mean, it's a Sunday morning right now. I can tell you that all across America last night young women were raped in fraternity houses. This is one area of college sexual assault that we can do something about, because these fraternities are organized groups and not just isolated individuals. But people are very loath to come up against the fraternity system.

KD: Why aren't the schools doing something about this?

CF: The first thing people always say is, "Colleges and universities should supervise those fraternities more and should have more chaperoning or monitoring of fraternity parties." But the colleges are extremely loath to do that because the more you supervise the fraternities, the more you establish a legal duty of care. The national administrations of the fraternities don't closely supervise the individual chapters for the same reason.

The national fraternity administrations argue—and there's some merit to what they're saying—they want the young men to be responsible for themselves. But it's a tremendous asset in a personal injury lawsuit against a fraternity if they can say, "We weren't responsible for that chapter on that campus. We gave them a strict set of rules. Whether or not they followed the rules was up to them."

KD: So why don't the schools just disassociate from the fraternities and kick them off campus?

CF: Colleges and universities have much more to gain from the fraternities than the fraternities have to gain from the colleges and universities. First, a school ties alumni to its campus in a very powerful way when it has a fraternity system. The more a school can get an alumnus back on campus, the more he or she is willing to write a check.

If you're an alumnus, and you want to go back at Homecoming weekend, and you want to have that great feeling you had as an undergraduate and kind of settle back in that life, if you weren't in a fraternity what are you going to go do? You can't knock on the door of your old dorm and say, "Hey guys, I lived here 30 years ago. Can I sit on your couch and, you know, have a beer and watch the game?"

But if you go to your fraternity house, you're going to be welcomed in. They've spent the two weeks before Homecoming getting the house ready for you. You're going to tell your war stories. You're going to point yourself out in the group photo on the wall. The fraternity makes you feel that you're still part of the institution. So for fundraising reasons, colleges have a lot invested in the fraternities.

Fraternities also provide a tremendous amount of student housing. One out of every eight college students living in college-related housing lives in Greek housing. That's a tremendous amount of housing stock the colleges don't have to raise money for, don't have to pay for, don't have to supervise. Finally, look at the boards of trustees of colleges and universities. Very often there are a number of wealthy men on those boards who are former fraternity men and probably had a great experience in their fraternity.

Most fraternity men aren't rapists. And most fraternity men aren't committing violent hazing. But the ones who do are causing tremendous misery for thousands of young people every year. Some people will say, better that the colleges have a formal relationship with the fraternities because then at least there's some oversight of the fraternities. I haven't found this argument to be true. One of the most shocking things I've found is that there will be rape after rape after rape at a fraternity house and nobody knows anything has happened there.

And when I go back to the University of Virginia, which I loved and where I got a great education, I will sometimes walk down Rugby Road where these beautiful old fraternity houses are.

I can look at them and acknowledge that they are very beautiful—they are historic. I can remember good times in a lot of them. But I look at them with a real chill because I know in nearly every one of those houses, young women have been raped year after year after year. And it has not changed at all since I was there in the early Eighties.

KD: Why don't the people who've devoted their lives to caring for young men and women—why don't they do something?
CF: Remember that the most well-funded political action committee [PAC] devoted exclusively to higher education is the fraternity PAC in Washington. They have poured money into making sure—at least in terms of public universities—that there is never any infringement on their right to freedom of association. Also, a large percentage of men in Congress were fraternity men themselves, and they get a substantial amount of money from fraternity lobbies and fraternity members. Nearly every time an education bill comes up for a reauthorization vote, Congress votes to make sure there are no restrictions placed on the fraternities.

KD: Why aren't we seeing college presidents stepping up to say, "I'm not going to let another several dozen women per year get raped on my campus?"
CF: What's the number-one responsibility of a college president? Fund-raising. You're going to alienate your fraternities and all the alumni giving that comes through former fraternity men?

KD: Have any college presidents tried to take this on?
CF: Amherst College has. They've closed down their fraternity system. We will see what comes of that. There can be an unintended

consequence that the fraternity is driven underground, and becomes an even more dangerous place.

People always say, "These young women—don't they know better?" I have a lot of compassion for these young women. They want to experience life. They feel themselves to be in every way the equal to the young men on campus. And they are equal, intellectually and athletically. So they see a lively party scene that's run by the fraternities and they want to be part of that, too. And remember, there is an incredible inequality in the Greek Life because sororities can't throw these big parties. Sororities can't serve alcohol. People drink alcohol in sorority houses, but you're never going to go by the sorority houses and find these open parties where kids are pouring in and out of the house and alcohol is being served.

KG: Why can't sororities have parties?

CF: I always say that when fraternities were founded in the nineteenth century, they were founded to protect young men from the feminizing aspects of education. And sororities were founded to protect young women from fraternity men. There was always this idea that the fraternity was a place where you were going to drink and play cards and maybe whore around a little bit. The fraternity is where you could "be a man"—you could have all that book learnin' but still be a man.

Traditionally, alcohol was not allowed at all in the sorority house and big open mixed parties weren't. That's been a tremendous benefit to the sorority industry because it has radically lowered their liability. Sorority parties happen outside the house, so all the risk is transferred onto the banquet hall or common room or the third-party provider of the alcohol. That's not to say terrible things don't happen at sorority events, but they don't happen anywhere near as much.

KD: What does happen at these fraternity parties? Can you sort of set the scene?

CF: What happens repeatedly around the country is a young woman goes to the fraternity and drinks. Now this young woman has every right to feel that she is in a safer space than the bar around the corner or a privately-owned house.

Why? Because every university has a whole web page devoted to their fraternities and their wonderful traditions. Her university tour guide took her on an exciting tour past Frat Row. She feels a level of safety that's not commensurate with what's often really going on at those fraternities. And her university knows the danger. Nearly every time there's a rape in a fraternity chapter, there's someone at the university who knows that chapter was likely to have a rape happen. But nobody tells the young woman.

So this young woman goes to the party. And suddenly she's had a couple of drinks and she looks around and she realizes, "There really aren't any more young women here. I'm the only one who's left here." And if she's a freshman she's putting this all together for the first time. And suddenly she's up against it with a young man who's very intent on having sex with her, and a nonconsensual sexual act takes place.

What's going to happen next? In most cases the woman does nothing. She feels a tremendous amount of shame and feels that, "Boy, I thought I was in with these guys. I guess I wasn't strong enough. I guess they didn't like me enough. Those other girls were smart enough to get out of that basement, and I wasn't smart enough."

Or maybe she reports it. I take reports of fraternity house rapes very seriously because it takes tremendous courage. You're not just coming into conflict with one young man who raped you. You are coming up against a brotherhood. That's their own language and they mean it. You're coming up against thirty or forty or seventy young men and they could all be in tremendous trouble if this rape gets exposed. You're coming up against a brotherhood of young men who have taken an oath of lifelong loyalty to one another. And if they are of a mind to make your life hell they will. Suddenly you're walking in the hallway to class: "Slut. Bitch." So usually the woman says nothing.

Then there's another rape at the fraternity house, and another, and another.

KD: What do you think should be done?

CF: Well the kneejerk response of many people is, "Those girls shouldn't go to those fraternity parties. Or if they do, they should be extremely careful not get too drunk, watch their drink so they don't get drugged, and have all their friends look out for each other." Let's think about the implications of that. We're saying that there's a huge industry operating freely on American campuses with the complete participation of the schools that is so dangerous that more than half of the student population either shouldn't go there at all, or they should go expecting something bad to happen. The fact that we, as a nation, are implicitly accepting this state of affairs is shocking and completely unacceptable.

KD: There has been some suggestion that making these fraternities co-ed would help.

CF: It's an interesting proposal, but it's really untested. It's similar to bystander intervention. We will know in five or six years if co-ed fraternities and bystander intervention works.

I'm all for people being aware this may happen and intervening if possible, but often that is not possible. For example, good luck if you're upstairs in a fraternity or in a basement and someone's locked the door. There aren't a lot of bystanders around at that moment. I wouldn't want a young woman to think she's safe because there are bystander intervention programs. I want her to *be* safe.

KD: Which fraternity do you think is doing it best?

CF: About 15 years ago Phi Delta Theta decided, "What are the two biggest problems on American college campuses? Alcohol and sexual assault. We should be leading in solving the problem, not in creating the problem." So they decided—a huge American fraternity—"We're going to have alcohol-free housing." Everybody said, "That's the end of that fraternity!" It has grown every single year in recruitment. The number of insurance claims against them for personal injury has dropped 85 percent and the dollar value of those claims has dropped 95 percent. There are bad chapters of Phi Delta Theta, just as there are of other fraternities, but Phi Delta Theta has made some very positive changes.

KD: Which are the worst fraternities?

CF: There's no such thing as a bad fraternity or a good fraternity. There are bad chapters and good chapters. It's also important to say that a lot of rapes that take place in fraternity houses are not committed by fraternity members or even by college students. Fraternity houses are very attractive places to marginal young men. Drug dealers will often hang out at fraternity houses.

KD: Can you talk a little bit about men and sexual assault?

CF: There is a significant amount of male sexual assault that goes on in fraternity houses, much of it under the guise of hazing. Hazing has always had a tremendously sexual element to it. Most fraternities claim they don't haze, and I believe they don't haze. Most fraternities that do haze—it doesn't involve anything extreme. But in fraternities that have a hazing problem, there are a lot of events that involve violent penetration.

KD: Can you talk about the benefits of being in a fraternity?
CF: There's a huge benefit to being in a fraternity. A woman whose son just graduated from college recently told me, "The fraternity saved my son." He got to college, he was so lonely, he couldn't make friends, and then second year he rushed the fraternity. He made the best friends of his life. The fraternity had been this incredible experience for her son.

They also offer [connections]. If you go to some regional school and you join the fraternity, suddenly you have connections. You know, you want to go into investment banking. You want to go into law. You want to go into politics. Suddenly you have this whole network that you never would've had access to otherwise.

KD: Where do you think we will be in 20 to 25 years on this issue?
CF: Exactly where we are now.

KD: Really? What is it going to take to change this?
CF: Litigation, I think, unfortunately.

Interview with Douglas Fierberg on the Power of Fraternities

Amy Ziering: Tell me about some of the college sexual assault cases you've worked on.

Doug Fierberg: I represented one woman who was sexually assaulted at a fraternity house. In the process we learned that that fraternity house had a history of sexual assault, but there was absolutely no way for women going to that school to find out that information.

AZ: But aren't there records?

DF: No. It's actually extremely difficult, if not impossible, to get accurate information about whether there have been sexual assaults in a particular fraternity house during the preceding years. So a lot of women go into certain fraternity houses without knowing they are dangerous places, and that the likelihood of getting sexually assaulted is far greater there than in most other locations on campus.

AZ: What are the conditions in fraternities that are conducive to these kinds of crimes?

DF: Let's start off with the reality that fraternities are essentially unregulated bars. They have a complete flow of alcohol on any given Friday or Saturday night, and the individuals who are responsible for managing the alcohol are themselves legally incapable of consuming it. So they're eighteen-, nineteen-, twenty-year-old kids who've never been trained in risk management, who are charged with the responsibility of serving a product that often gets people extremely intoxicated and in many circumstances leads to injury and death. And it's not only sexual violence against women, but there are many circumstances that involve third-party liability. For example, situations where someone drinks too much, leaves the fraternity house, and gets in a car accident. Fraternities are the top risk facing young people on college campuses.

AZ: And insurers know this and continue to insure fraternities?
DF: Well, the way they're insured is also a bit of a sham. The insurance premiums are paid out of the dues of individual members so that if there are numerous claims against the fraternity because of sexual assault, all the fraternity does is raise the membership dues.

AZ: Does that work?
DF: Yes, it works, historically. Most fraternities have never been hit hard financially for the harm that they've been involved in causing, because they simply insure against the risk, and they pass those insurance premiums on to students, whose rates have increased 200, 300—even 400 percent in the last 10 years.

AZ: Do the insurance companies keep records of all these claims?
DF: Yes, but getting at that information is extremely difficult. We've fought that industry two or three times to get the risk history and the loss history so we could demonstrate how much the fraternities know about the possibility of risk for women who go to events at fraternities. And they've fought us constantly to keep that information from becoming public.

And so if you're a woman, for example, going to a particular university, you cannot find any publicly-available information about fraternity houses on campus. For example, at the University of Minnesota, I believe it was about three years ago, they had between three and nine sexual assaults in certain fraternity houses during one fall semester. If you were a woman on that college campus, you may have heard a mention of one of those assaults on the news, but if you went to the university's website there would be no mention of that history of assaults at those fraternities.

AZ: And what about the universities—do they disclose this information?

DF: No, they don't tell the truth. What you find in many circumstances is that universities have created contractual relationships with fraternities that involve them promoting the fraternities, but not disclosing the risks. So for example, you can go into your average university website, and you'll see "Go Greek!" Or you'll see promotional materials for what it means to be Greek on campus. Occasionally they'll even do FAQs—frequently asked questions— that address risk issues, but then quell your concerns by saying "You've heard about *Animal House*, you've seen stories here and there, but that's not true on our college campus." When in fact it may be very true.

AZ: Can you describe the fraternity structure? Who oversees them, who do they report to, who makes sure they're being responsible?

DF: There's a national structure, most often incorporated in Indiana for tax reasons, and then under that structure they may have chapter corporations, or housing corporations, that manage the affairs at the college campus. And so the chapter may be managed by eighteen-, nineteen-year-old kids who have just been elected president, vice president, or risk manager for the chapter. It's a popularity contest, and as a result of popularity, you now have someone charged with managing the risk of the fraternity at the local level. The national group will send leadership consultants around on a semi-annual basis to take a look at the chapter and provide some education, but they often don't want to do that too much because they feel like they're exposing themselves to liability.

AZ: They're exposing themselves to liability by training people to act responsibly?
DF: Yes. They believe that they're exposing themselves to potential liability if they act reasonably to educate the students and to make sure that what they're doing is actually safe. It's easier for them to avoid liability by saying, "We're disconnected from our local operations. All we do is provide them with educational materials and if they choose to follow those educational materials, that's their decision."

AZ: Has that been working for them in terms of escaping liability?
DF: It used to work. But we've sort of punched a hole in that and kept some fraternities from becoming absolved of responsibility on those very grounds.

AZ: Are you finding in your lawsuits that there's a financial settlement, but no behavioral change?
DF: We have been insisting on behavioral change at all of the organizations we've sued. So, for example, when we had a death case out in California recently, we required that the national fraternity put

it on its website, so students and parents can look at this information, including all of the locations in the preceding five years where members have been suspended or expelled as a result of risk management violations. That mere disclosure is twenty pages long.

In our litigation, when we're settling or resolving a matter with a national fraternity, we insist upon what we call "non-economic changes," things that the organization has to do in order to make it safe in the future for other people.

AZ: But if they have an endless source of cash and are protected by huge insurance policies, what is going to finally compel them to change?

DF: It's not an easy problem to solve, but the only way to begin solving the problem is using the judicial system. Because legislatively, something like 60 percent of U.S. Congressmen are fraternity members, so it's very difficult to get any sort of legislative solution that would solve the problem of fraternity misconduct. So the only answer right now is using the power through the judicial process.

AZ: When you file these cases against a fraternity, how do they respond?

DF: One of the first things they start doing is looking to see if they can blame the victim. They look at the circumstances of how the sexual assault took place, and if it in any way involves poor judgment on the part of the victim, they focus on that.

AZ: And what are the effects of that on your clients?

DF: It's devastating for them, but we've prepared them in advance. One of the things that helps women is when the lawsuit is not just about money, it's also about causing change. They can cause changes by entering into a settlement that requires things to be done that will help other women in the future.

AZ: What do you think impedes this information from coming out?

DF: Universities cite federal privacy law, called FERPA. They argue that FERPA requires them to keep a lot of this information confidential, and that's just not true. FERPA requires that you keep the name of the perpetrator and the victim confidential, and perhaps other identifiable student information, but it doesn't mean the incident itself is confidential. So you can publicly report that there have been sexual assaults at the Alpha Beta Gamma fraternity, and that doesn't involve privacy issues. But they won't even go as far as to report that.

AZ: Why not?

DF: You'd have to ask them. There's absolutely no rational reason for keeping this information secret.

AZ: Do these fraternities push back very hard against you?

DF: Constantly. They are of the view that if they consistently defend the cases and defend them with a scorched-earth approach, that ultimately it will take the advocate in me away from the victims. Because if it's not an easy remedy, if it's too costly for the victim, it will discourage a woman from bringing a civil claim. And that's right out of their playbook. The fraternities made a mistake a number of years ago by putting out on a website the playbook developed by their lawyers. One of the strategies in the playbook is to make the litigation expensive for plaintiffs' attorneys to coordinate litigation with other defendants. They posted this online and *Bloomberg News* found it and we found it as well.

AZ: What keeps you going?

DF: Passion. This is the right thing to do. It's the right thing to do for the right people. And if you look at some traditions of law where the justice system has been used independent of the legislature to create change, there's a tremendous legacy of that. You can go back to *Brown v. Board of Education*. You can go back to a woman's right to informed consent about what's done to [her body] in surgery. Most of that tradition came out of the judicial system. It's a good fight.

AZ: When you first started getting these cases, were you surprised by what you found?

DF: Yes. The first two cases I had in the school setting was a woman who was set up to be raped by an acquaintance in high school and a fraternity hazing case. I learned how significant these issues were at schools, and that there was no coordinated set of lawyers that represented victims. But there was a coordinated set of defense lawyers who had been defending these cases for years and were poised to eliminate a woman's effort to get her rights fully prosecuted.

For example, in California there's a go-to lawyer who has been representing fraternities for years. He has access to institutional information across the country that fraternities have been using to defend these cases. He has access to the information of many defense lawyers who have been representing fraternities for years. In addition, he has access to the lawyers in Indiana or Ohio who have helped fraternities protect themselves, from a corporate perspective, to reduce their exposure.

AZ: What would you want people watching this film to know?

DF: Send your young family members to college with your eyes wide open. Make sure that you understand that there are substantial risks at universities, particularly with fraternities, for your daughters or young women you care about. Make sure that they clearly understand that when they go to fraternity houses on Friday and Saturday nights, they have to pay attention and not be separated from their friends. They should go there with friends and leave with friends. I've told my daughters the same thing. Of course, we shouldn't have to warn young women about how to protect themselves from the young men at the colleges and universities. We should be educating our young men so that they don't do this, and investigating and prosecuting the men who do. But we have a long way to go before we get there.

AZ: Many of the women I've interviewed have said, "I did do the right thing, but it still happened."
DF: I know. The easiest solution—although it's often not practicable because fraternities now have such a large social presence on most university campuses—is just not go at all. But you're not at fault if you do go and you are assaulted. You need to take extra precautions, and it still doesn't mean that you're going to be safe.

AZ: Can you talk a little bit about the way that alcohol is used in fraternities?
DF: If you think about the way alcohol's managed in this country, you cannot go to your average bar or restaurant without there being a bar manager, and some governmental oversight as to how the alcohol is served. Your average bar on the street corner has a manager. That manager probably had to get licensed by an alcohol beverage control board. At fraternities, there's absolutely no oversight. They serve alcohol regularly on Friday and Saturday nights— often Thursday nights and Wednesday nights as well. And there's

no oversight. You have eighteen- and nineteen-year-olds managing the operation, making decisions about whether or not someone's going to be served.

Fraternities are outside the normal level of control that universities place on student housing. Fraternities house the highest risk population—young men, eighteen- to nineteen-year-olds—the population insurance industry information says is at the highest risk for binge drinking. That's who's living in and managing fraternities.

AZ: What is the impact on the families of students who have been assaulted?

DF: It's devastating. They've shared the dreams of their child who is going off to school—and then they get a terrifying phone call. And then they're facing a circumstance where their child is depressed, in counseling, lost, trying to figure things out. It's just devastating. They want their child back. They want their child to have their hopes and dreams and be able to accomplish the things that she set off to do. They want their child strong again, confident. Not victimized, not apologetic for circumstances that were not her fault.

AZ: Do you think these crimes can be reduced?

DF: Yes, absolutely. They can't be eliminated, but they can be dramatically reduced. One simple solution would be to make fraternity houses dry. If you pulled the alcohol out of fraternity houses (and fraternities know this, because this information is available to them) that would reduce the prevalence of injury and death by 98 percent.

AZ: What makes you angriest about all this?

DF: Young people are being hurt for no reason, and no one is stopping it. And when you try to talk to them about stopping it, you're dealing with insular male groups who haven't had anybody force them to change in decades. Get rid of the alcohol and you'll save countless women. I think they believe that if they took the alcohol out of the houses, their very raison d'être would be gone, because they're taking away places where people can party without supervision. And if they lose membership, they'd lose money.

AZ: What about just regulating alcohol consumption by having an adult there?

DF: Well, that costs money, too. Fraternities, historically, had a house mother, a mature individual who would look at a situation and say, "Stop serving," or, "She needs help; someone should take her to the hospital." That management system was taken out in the sixties. So you could change things by either making fraternities dry or putting in responsible management. And both of these cost money. That's the one financial commitment the national fraternity organizations will not make.

They did a 10-year study on one fraternity that had gone dry, and the statistics show that they would reduce injury and death substantially by this one change. As I understand it, the fraternity did not lose membership. There were a number of young men who were interested in joining an organization that followed the principles that it purportedly stood for: academics, community service, things like that, as opposed to having a party-animal atmosphere.

AZ: You would think that the senior management in at least some of the fraternities would take this on.

DF: It's very difficult for national fraternities to make these changes because of the way they are set up. They're membership organizations, and their constitutions have empowered their student members with a certain amount of control over the organization. Even if the national senior management puts forward a motion that the fraternity be alcohol-free, that motion can be voted down by their eighteen- to twenty-two-year-old student members. So even in the infrequent cases when senior management recognizes the risk and puts forth a motion, their undergraduate members have nearly always voted that down.

AZ: What specific legislation would you like to see passed to address this issue?
DF: I think all Greek housing should be subject to the same rules and regulations as all other student housing, and subject to the same university oversight. That would go great lengths to bringing more mature supervision to Greek housing.

AZ: That seems logical. Why don't legislatures do that?
DF: I'm not sure the public understands the risk. Before social change can take place, the public has to become aware of what's wrong. The public doesn't know that just one insurance broker for the fraternities has handled six thousand claims and 60 million dollars in payouts for injury and death across the country. And that's just one broker. Until the public understands how dangerous these organizations can be, you can't expect there to be legislative change.

AZ: What will it take to change things?
DF: I don't know. Perhaps an extreme tragedy beyond the tragedies we've already seen. Something in the range of what happened at Virginia Tech, where it absolutely shocks the conscience; something where the public says, "No more of this. This has to end!"

AZ: And where do you think we'll be thirty years from now?
DF: Hopefully not in the same position we are right now, where so many women are hurt, needlessly, on college campuses. Hopefully we'll advance justice for women in the next thirty years.

Before the Frat Party

Amy Ziering joined three University of California. Berkeley students as they gathered at their student co-op (similar to a dorm) to get ready for a night out. The women spoke candidly to Amy about the frat party scene— from the dress code, Jell-O shots, and "walk of shame," to the horrors of sexual assault.

Amy: What parties are you going to?
Jordan: So there's a house that is pretty much right next door to us—two houses down—it's Phi Psi and they're like a tiny frat, and we're probably not gonna get in unless we go really early and no one's there because you have to have a bid, which is like an invite.

Amy: What's the criteria for getting in?
Emma: You usually have to know someone in the frat, you have to be a girl, and you kind of have to be attractive.

Amy: Wait—they decide based on how you look?
Jordan: Yeah. My roommate Hannah has a British accent and she's a very attractive young lady and we'll usually push her forward to talk to the guys because—
Emma:—you have a better chance that way.
Jordan: She almost always gets us in.

Amy: How does that make you guys feel?
Jordan: I don't think too much of it.

Aryle: Sometimes the frats have a certain ratio of women to men in the frat parties.

Emma: You need a high ratio of girls in your group if you want to get in.

Jordan: Ideally, no guys. They don't want to let guys in, if you're a group of girls, then guys will just approach you on the street and they're like, "Hey! You wanna be friends with me? Like, come on! Let's go together!" And they start getting all buddy-buddy.

Emma: If guys try to get in by themselves, they won't.

Jordan: And when you get inside it's almost all women and then the brothers of the frat. Like, almost no one else. It's pretty intimidating when it's just like the brothers and you're almost like—I feel like prey sometimes. Like, you're being hunted.

Emma: I feel very objectified. I feel like I can't leave the circle or else I'll have guys surrounding me in five seconds.

Jordan: Yeah. It's definitely a little intimidating to feel like prey.

Emma: It's not even intimidating, it's kind of scary.

Amy: What's the pleasure here? Why do it?

Emma: I don't understand it when I think about it now. The pleasure was not in going out, the pleasure was in getting ready to go out and coming back from going out—

Amy: The party itself, what does that feel like?

Emma: We try to go to dance and then there'll be points where we don't find good music so we'll just stand there and kind of not do anything.

Amy: Are there any parties where guys don't judge you before walk in?

Emma: No.

Jordan: I can't really think of one. At the door is when you really feel it. When you're trying to negotiate and almost to the point where you're pulling down your top like, "Look, I have boobs. And objectify me so I can get in." And then you get in.

Emma: To somewhere you don't even really want to go just because you feel like you need to get in.

Amy: Has it ever occurred to the women to just organize and not go to these parties?

Jordan: It's a social ranking. You say, "Well, what'd you do this weekend?" "Oh, I went to this frat, and this frat," and so saying that you got in, not only does it say so much about your attractiveness but also it's like . . . they approve of me.

I mean, it seems so compulsory. There's something that's like ingrained, especially when you're in the dorm. There seems to be this invisible pressure for us to go out to all the frats every weekend.

Amy: Do you choose your clothes based on what you feel like wearing or what you feel like will get you in someplace?

Jordan: It's definitely been fifty degrees out and I've put on this number, which is basically nothing and I was freezing. And I don't know why. Well, I do know why—'cause I wanted to get into the party. If I was going to wear what I wanted to wear, I would be in my fuzzy socks. I would be in a big jacket.

Amy: So you have to show skin.

Jordan: That's the general rule.

Emma: You have to keep pulling down your dress the whole time when you're dancing and making sure your bra's not showing and . . .

Aryle: When you pull it up you show your butt.

Emma: Yeah! Now you're like, how do I cover all my parts?

Amy: Was this normal for you in high school?

Jordan: No. I didn't go out at all in high school.

Emma: I didn't either. The first time we'd been exposed to this was in college.

Amy: Did you feel objectified by guys like this in high school?

Jordan: No, but, if I'm being honest, I never got attention from guys in high school like that. Although it's disappointing to be objectified, when you get in there and you're being hit on by guy after guy after guy, it's like, "Okay, yeah! I am attractive." Somehow you're reaffirming your self-confidence through these guys that—

Emma: You're not gonna hook up with them, you're not gonna do anything with them; they just come up to you almost like a piece of meat and they think that it's okay to just hit on you.

Jordan: When we're dancing—not twerking like Miley Cyrus or anything—just dancing, a guy'll be coming up behind you and he won't be like, "Oh, hey, how are you?" or like, "My name's so-and-so." They just go and grab your hips. So we have a system where I'll see a guy coming up and we'll say: "God, my boyfriend's gonna get here soon and he'll—"

Emma: "He's a __ player! His arms are this big."

Jordan: We've come up with systems because it gets to the point where you're kinda harassed and you're like, *Do I even get to look the guy in the eye who's like grinding on me right now?* I've definitely danced with a guy for 10 minutes and not had any idea what he looked like.

Emma: Yeah, you have to judge from your friend's reaction to see who's dancing behind you.

Jordan: Give me a 1 to 10. How bad is this right now?

Amy: Do you guys ever feel unsafe inside the party?

Jordan: I don't think I've ever been by myself in the party. I usually have a couple of my friends.

Emma: You can't be by yourself. Because . . . ? You just don't. If a guy comes up to you that you haven't met and tries to dance with you, you always have that out if you have a girl with you.

Jordan: And you always have someone to help you not make stupid decisions. We [went out with] one of our floor-mates, and she drank more than I thought, and then four of us walked back and she wasn't with us. And we got back and her roommate said, "Oh, where's so-and-so?" And I was like, "Still at the party, I guess."

Emma: We walked back in our pajamas at 2 in the morning and knocked on every single door upstairs until we found her and brought her home.

Jordan: I had to coerce my way into that frat. I was like, "You're letting me in. I don't care if I'm in sweats. I need to get in there right now." I found her in one of the rooms with three guys.

Amy: So, if you guys ruled the world, what would you like parties to be like?

Emma: I know my perfect party would just be music. Just great music.

Jordan: And people hanging out.

Emma: And they'd all be people that I knew, friends of friends. Because that way everybody gets filtered.

Jordan: The idea that a complete stranger—many complete strangers—are at this party, and going in and out constantly gets pretty scary. I mean, there's very few parties that actually check for student IDs, so you don't even necessarily have to be a student.

Amy: At the parties, do guys talk to you?

Jordan: No. I don't think I've ever had a discussion where it's like, "What's your major?"

Emma: Never. You can't even start to dance with a guy because if you start to dance with a guy then it's assumed that you're gonna do everything else with that man. It's almost like a contract.

Jordan: We've talked about that a lot this year: Why do we feel so obligated? Like, just because we let some guy start dancing with us—consent was not given to dance with me. Ever. No one walked up to me and asked for my name and asked if they could dance with me, let alone grind on me. And then for some reason, once that happens, I feel guilty . . .

Aryle: I've heard guys complain like, "I danced with her for like a whole 30 minutes and she just left."

Jordan: That's why I feel guilty. I've heard guys say to their guy friends, "Yeah, she didn't even put out and we made out on the couch next to the dance floor for a half an hour."

Emma: It shouldn't be: We kiss, now we can go all the way. I feel like I'm in a fifties movie.

Amy: Do you ever expect the guys to wear something? Do they dress for the party?

Jordan: We've ranted about this. They wear cargo pants and a T-shirt.

Emma: They don't try at all.

Amy: How is alcohol used?

Jordan: One of the reasons we go to this one frat is that they have alcohol and a lot of it and it's easy to get. And that was one of our main motivators last year as freshmen. It's alcohol everywhere. You usually just have to be like, "Where is the handle?" Or like, "Where are the Jell-O shots?" A nice young man will be like, "Oh, it's back there!" And then you have it.

Amy: Have you ever seen any a woman in trouble or in a questionable situation and you're worried about her?

Jordan: At probably every party I saw a girl being led upstairs.

Emma: Yeah, you don't go upstairs with a brother of the frat unless you're gonna have sex with him. That is the rule for upstairs. It's almost like if you go into a frat party, every guy there assumes that you're there to hook up with one of them.

Jordan: It's always the guys who get to choose and they just walk up to us and talk to us and "Oh, well, he's ugly, I guess I have to talk to him." That sucks.

Emma: You feel obligated. And it's not like we get to say "I'm not attracted to you so please go away."

Amy: Why not? Who wrote these rules?

Jordan: I don't know.

Emma: The weird part is nobody tells you about this. You just kind of know when you walk in.

Jordan: And then you feel so accomplished when you're like, "Yeah, I'm a freshman and I went to all these frats 'cause I'm figuring out the system and I know how to get in." It's like a stepping-stone as a freshman. You're like, "Yeah, this is like college life."

Emma: A rite of passage. This is what you do in college.

Amy: Okay, so you get dressed up, you put makeup on, if you get in you're happy 'cause you got accepted. If you get rejected, how do people feel?

Jordan: That sucks.

Emma: In a dress. In makeup. We never wear makeup. Now we have on makeup. What are we gonna do?

Jordan: So you're like, "Now let's just go back to the dorm because I'm tired of being rejected." It's a terrible feeling.

Emma: My friend who's a guy and he's gay, he tried to get into a frat party by himself and they said, "No, no, no, no, no." But then he said, "I'm gay." And they completely changed, pulled out a huge stack of wristbands, slapped one on his wrist, they all slapped him on the back and he was in. And it was because he was gay, and he wasn't going to take any of the women.

Amy: But weren't they worried he might hit on a frat guy?

Emma: I feel like they like women more than they're afraid of getting hit on by a man.

Aryle: And also too, women often feel a little bit safer around gay men. You have a couple of gay men at a frat party, the women are a little more likely to relax, so it makes it easier to give a woman a bunch of alcohol because she's like, "Oh, he's just gay."

Jordan: And then there's the Corner of Darkness. The Corner of Darkness is four frats that are all fairly close to each other that have built a reputation for sexual assault.

Emma: They have a reputation for date-raping girls. If you go in, you run that risk.

Jordan: But it has the reverse effect, which is the weirdest thing. There're so many stories about one of those frats. "This happened to this girl. This guy did this." But still women are like, "Oh my god, but can we go there tonight?"

Emma: You're kind of curious.

Jordan: It has the worst reputation and it's the most exclusive frat. It's well known for making women uncomfortable and you want to get into it the most. It's crazy.

Emma: We have a few friends in that frat and it boggles our minds because they seem like perfectly nice people, but they rushed the frat anyway. They knew that people were getting date-raped and they still wanted to pledge. And I don't understand why.

Jordan: From our balcony we can watch freshman stumble inebriated down the street in high heels on their way to these frats.

Aryle: And then in the morning watch girls walk back holding their heels.

Jordan: It's called "the walk of shame." I've sat on my balcony and watched the walk of shame: That's heels in hand, your hair's messed up, and you have makeup under your eyes.

Aryle: Sometimes you wanna ask, "Are you okay?" I'm pretty sure those girls are, but then there's always those girls that don't remember.

Jordan: That has to be so scary.

Emma: And even if they gave consent to that at the time it doesn't count. You're so drunk.

Jordan: Yeah. I've felt comfortable hooking up with a guy and then I've stayed over, and the next morning you don't feel okay. It's actually termed "the walk of shame." Even if I made my own decision, alcohol or not, if I'm walking back in the morning with shoes in hand, in this dress or whatever, it's literally the walk of shame.

5

Contributing Essays

For this book, we reached out to writers and thinkers from around the country and asked them to respond to *The Hunting Ground*. Our contributors include university professors, journalists, writers, film experts, and anti-assault activists, each of whom shares their own unique take on the film. All of our contributors were familiar with the issue of sexual violence: Some work with women and men who have been assaulted, others have seen the effects on people they love, a few are survivors themselves. One writer takes a close-up look at the culture of college athletics, another examines how the media handles sexual assault post–*Rolling Stone*, a third considers *The Hunting Ground* in the context of contemporary documentaries, still another discusses what it means to watch the film as a man. Together, their thoughtful and diverse points of view amount to a collective call for action.

Not the Perfect Victim

by Kamilah Willingham

There's now a national spotlight on the issue of campus sexual assault: award-winning filmmakers and authors have devoted themselves to the issue, joining students' demands for change. State and national lawmakers are responding to the issue; even the White House is on board. This is an incredible moment, and there's so much we can do with it. Of course, we still have a *very* long way to go, but looking at how far we've come, I feel like we can accomplish anything.

I found my home in the anti-violence movement *before* I was sexually assaulted. There were times when I felt that I couldn't—or shouldn't—do the work, because it was too personal. But then I realized it was *always* personal. We've all encountered, to varying degrees, glaring injustices. Many of us have found ourselves facing or even standing right in the middle of some outrageous cultural blind spots.

I'm now working at the California Women's Law Center, surrounded by people who inspire me. Before I came to this position, I worked for Just Detention International (JDI) on a very specific issue: prisoner rape. Before I applied for that job, I didn't know much about the issue. I knew that it happened; I knew that it was treated as a punch line. One of the things that struck me the most at JDI was the sheer volume of survivors of sexual assault in detention, some of whom are in situations of ongoing abuse, who are *desperate* to tell their stories—desperate to be heard. What gave *me* the courage to share my story was knowing that people were finally listening. While JDI gives prisoners hope that some people are listening, we know it's not the same, right? We have a long way to go before prisoners who have been sexually abused are afforded the same visibility, the same outrage, as college students who have been sexually abused.

It's a terrible truth, but one that I can't afford to ignore: All survivors are not created—or treated—equally. Some people's stories are privileged over others.

In my case, for example, I was assaulted while attending an extremely elite institution. I was a Harvard Law student. My assailant was a Harvard Law student. What became painfully clear to me when I was working with prisoners is that people tend to care much more about what happens in elite spaces.

If I wasn't a Harvard Law School student, I don't know if anyone would have listened to my story, because in no way did I fit the notion of the perfect victim. I drank, I danced, I did drugs, I flirted. I didn't respond to my assault like a "perfect victim"— because who knows what that means these days? I didn't kick, scream, say no three times, and click my heels together. And I'm fully aware that those factors make me—in some people's eyes—responsible, at least in part, for what happened. For being attacked by a person I considered a friend, in my own apartment.

After I was assaulted, I showed my anger. It was only later that I realized that many people are more inclined to believe the plight of a "broken" victim. Even now, there's a little voice in my head saying, "Shut up, Kamilah! You're gonna lose your credibility if you show that you're angry." But I can't shut up. I'm sick of the notion that we have to pull back on our agency, shrink down our identities, so that we can fit into this little box that represents what an innocent, truly sympathetic victim supposedly looks like.

Every time a black person gets shot or "mysteriously" dies in police custody, our hearts sink. And we barely have the chance to begin to process our collective grief before the inevitable questions in the media start coming: *Was he a marijuana user? Why was she provoking the officer? Didn't he have a history of run-ins with the law?*

This is how oppression works. Certain people are painted as complicit in their own victimization—complicit or just asking for it by virtue of who they are—because there's this brutal reluctance to acknowledge what happens to "others." It's far easier to silence them.

We have to keep in mind that political movements, especially highly charged ones, have a way of fracturing. We need to guard against that fracturing by embracing and appreciating our differences, and seeking understanding of experiences we may not relate to. We know that no one can do this work alone. We know that you can't fight rape in a vacuum, because rape doesn't occur in a vacuum. If you address sexual assault as an issue in and of itself, rather than considering it in the context in which it occurs, you will never cease marginalizing certain people. If we are to create change that refuses to leave out the people who are too often left out of the social justice movement, we need to embrace the complexity of sexual assault, the circumstances in which it occurs, and the people it affects.

Because of the work of the activists, scholars, and incredible leaders who have paved the way, I believe that this young, loud, and empowered generation of activists knows that you can't truly address, understand, or effectively fight sexual assault—or any outrage—without addressing the intersecting layers of oppression that enable this violence and silence its victims. Thanks to the pioneers who came before us, this is a generation that grew up with the language of intersectionality. I think the new wave of activists are fed up with strategic silences and are fighting hard to build inclusive and lasting movements.

Right now, the work of activists has landed us in an incredibly politically fortunate moment. People who have been sexually assaulted are, more and more, speaking out about their experiences—and what's amazing about this moment is that *the world seems to actually be listening.* The momentum that these amazing men and women have built is stunning. More and more people are willing to share the burden of sexual assault victims' pain and outrage, and to fight for change. In the past, it must have seemed impossible that the public would take on this fight, but it's happening now before our eyes.

For example, several years ago, a number of women came forward and said Bill Cosby sexually assaulted them. It was barely a footnote in his career—no one listened. Then we came to this moment. A couple more women came forward, and they empowered and inspired a few more, and now I've lost count of the dozens of women standing together, telling their stories, demanding recognition of what happened to them and so many others.

It means something that we're hearing so many survivors' voices. And the more we hear, the more other survivors feel comfortable coming forward, too. There are those who will attack us, try to knock us down, invalidate our experiences. But you *can't* invalidate all of us. There is strength in numbers.

At the same time, I want this to be a distinct moment in history. We're feeling strong enough to "come out" as survivors, to share our experiences with the public, and I think that's a powerful moment to recognize. But it shouldn't take "seeing" or "knowing" someone who's been raped for us to care. We shouldn't have to sacrifice privacy and open ourselves up to public scrutiny in order to validate the experiences of one in five women.

For the record, I'm still angry. A lot of us in this room are still angry. We have a lot of reasons to be angry. It's a turn-off for some, but I've learned to embrace that anger—it means we don't accept the status quo; it means that we expect our culture and our institutions to do better. My anger makes me strong and makes me bold, and that's what I see in a lot of today's activists. It may not be palatable to some, but I don't think we care. We're ready to move away from the "perfect victim" framework.

A luta continua—the struggle continues. But we're in good company!

Adapted from Kamilah Willingham's September 2015 keynote speech at the opening session of the National Sexual Assault Conference in Los Angeles. Willingham, one of the sexual assault survivors who appears in The Hunting Ground, *now works at the California Women's Law Center, a nonprofit organization that advances the potential of women and girls through litigation, policy advocacy, and education.*

Dispatch from Hunted Ground

by Roxane Gay

I have spent most of my life on the hunting ground, as an undergrad, a graduate student, and now, a professor. I am, I suppose, one of the lucky ones. The campuses where I've spent my time, particularly as a student, have never felt like a hunting ground. I've been able to attend classes, or not on my less responsible days when sleeping in felt like the better choice. I partied. I made regrettable but consensual choices. I made awesome and consensual choices. I somehow avoided becoming a campus assault statistic. I learned, and made mistakes, and had invaluable experiences and grew, and now I teach and work with students from the other side.

The hunting ground where I was raped, at twelve years old, was the woods behind the neighborhood where my family lived. I was gang raped in an abandoned hunting cabin, by boys I went to school with, boys I thought I knew. I didn't know I was on a hunting ground until I knew, and then there was no escape. In some ways, I am still trapped there. This is, I suppose, what lucky looks like.

As I watched *The Hunting Ground,* as I bore witness to the testimony of young women and men who have been sexually assaulted on college campuses, I thought of how egregiously these students were failed by institutions that are, at their best, designed to help those same students find their way into the world. I recognized that victims of campus sexual assault all too often have no escape from the ground where they were hunted unless they choose to leave their school.

I was stunned by the documentary, though I am not sure why.

Certainly, I knew there was a problem with sexual violence on college campuses. Whenever there is a sexual assault at my university, I receive an email that reads, *ALERT: Campus police investigate sexual assault report.* Details, if there are any, follow: where the assault happened, what the suspect looks like. We are urged, as members of the campus community, to come forward if we have information.

I travel to dozens of college campuses to speak each year. When I am being driven around I am shown where, for example, a young woman was raped while people stood around videotaping the incident on their cell phones. I meet with groups of students who say, "Have you heard . . .?" and I listen as they tell me of recent campus assaults, of their outrage at being ignored by administrators, of their fear of being prey rather than students.

There are the national statistics that never seem to improve. On September 21, 2015, the American Association of Universities released a report of the largest survey on sexual assault on college and university campuses ever conducted. There were more than 150,000 respondents, and the report largely told us what we already know: One in four undergraduate women will experience some kind of sexual violence during her college years. The report also indicated that victims of sexual assault are reluctant to come forward. They don't necessarily trust university administrators to support their best interests. Among students themselves, nearly half of the respondents indicated that there were times when they did not intervene when they witnessed some kind of sexual violence.

There are the people who try to refute these statistics, who prefer to interrogate methodologies and terminologies and testimonies rather than to accept the gravity of the very real problem we are facing.

Perhaps it is the gravity of the problem, as it was so relentlessly, powerfully depicted throughout *The Hunting Ground* that left me stunned. To see so many young women and men who had been assaulted on what should have been safe ground, to see how little justice they were afforded, was a painful reminder of the extent of rape culture and the work we have ahead of us in combating that culture.

There is plenty of blame to go around for this campus rape epidemic, but it is too easy to simply dismiss the prevalence of sexual violence on campus as a by-product of an overly arrogant, unchecked athletic culture on college campuses, or a Greek system gone wild, though both of these things are true. It is too easy to dismiss this sexual violence as a necessary by-product of the permissiveness and loosened inhibitions that rise out of unfettered access to alcohol and drugs.

But we need to do more than assign blame. We cannot assume that there is a convenient profile of the college students committing sexual assault. It's not just entitled athletes or fraternity members committing these crimes. It is students from all walks of life. We need to acknowledge that our culture is raising young men and women who have no understanding of consent. Our culture is raising young men and women who don't step up and intervene when they see someone vulnerable being preyed upon.

When I look at my students, I see witty, intelligent, generally charming young people who make my life so very interesting. But I worry that I am not looking closely enough. When they leave my classroom or my office or that moment when we see each other on campus pathways, I know little of their lives. I worry that I don't see predators or prey. I wonder if I should.

While watching *The Hunting Ground* I considered, time and again, the role faculty should play in addressing sexual violence on campus. I was particularly surprised to see so little said by tenured faculty who have the job security to speak up for students and to challenge administrations that protect perpetrators and university reputations rather than victims of sexual assault. I don't have easy answers for what we should do, but I know we cannot continue to remain silent. We cannot care, but only do so passively. We need to act, aggressively.

As college professors, our job is to teach students from our given area of expertise, but it is clearly also time for us, regardless of what we are assigned to teach, to instruct our students in the ways of humanity. If we do nothing to try and address sexual violence on the campuses where we teach, we are, with our silence, issuing permits for sexual predators to roam freely on the hunting grounds of our campuses.

Roxane Gay is a writer and professor whose work has appeared in Best American Mystery Stories 2014, Best American Short Stories 2012, Best Sex Writing 2012, A Public Space, McSweeney's, Tin House, Oxford American, *and many others. She is the co-editor of* PANK. *She is also the author of* Ayiti, An Untamed State, Bad Feminist, *and* Hunger. *She is a professor of English at Purdue University.*

Watching While Male:
Why Campus Assault Is an Urgent Men's Issue

by Andrew O'Hehir

I can only imagine that for many women, seeing Kirby Dick and Amy Ziering's documentary *The Hunting Ground* was an experience that came with immense relief, and tremendous validation. As we have seen more recently with the allegations against, for example, Bill Cosby, there is strength in public solidarity, and the sheer number of young women who come forward in *The Hunting Ground* to tell their stories of rape or sexual assault on college campuses from coast to coast—appearing on camera and using their full names—will change the nature of the issue for any viewer. Of course we, the audience, cannot know whether every individual story is true in detail, but in the face of all that testimony the cloak of epistemological murk our culture has often thrown over the issue of rape in general and campus rape in particular becomes unsustainable.

For a male viewer—which of course was my only possible perspective—*The Hunting Ground* poses a challenge. All these heart-wrenching, enraging, and courageous personal histories, some delivered with wit, others in tears, and others with steely determination, demand of men whether we have done enough to prevent these crimes, and countless others, from happening. Unfortunately, only one answer is possible. This is first and foremost a film about young women and men claiming their own power, but it is mostly men who commit rape, and in the long run it is men who can help stop it.

This is not a challenge all men will welcome, to say the least. But self-flagellation about the evils of masculinity is decidedly not the point, and neither is a collective defense mechanism like the #NotAllMen that emerged after the Isla Vista massacre near the UC Santa Barbara campus in 2014. No one is claiming that all men commit crimes of sexual violence, or even a large proportion of men. While the true force of the film does not lie in statistical evidence, the social science data on this question is fairly clear. Most rapes are committed by a core group of repeat offenders, no larger than 3 to 4 percent of the male population.

I do not imagine that many men in that subset of the population are likely to see the film *The Hunting Ground,* or read this book and feel penitent, although one should never rule out the possibilities of human change and redemption. But the film lays down its challenge before the other 96 to 97 percent of us, men who have never sexually assaulted a woman and almost certainly never will, but who have tolerated a gender-defined cloud of confusion and denial around this whole question for too long. I feel some ambivalence about the feminist-theory term "rape culture" (which is not used in the film), but that's what it refers to: Our society has ignored, denied, and willfully misinterpreted an entire class of violent crime, which occurs everywhere but appears to be distressingly common in the hothouse atmosphere of college life, and has depicted it as some sort of impenetrable mystery, where ultimate truth cannot be known.

End Rape on Campus, the ingenious activist movement formed by University of North Carolina rape survivors Annie Clark and Andrea Pino, is first and foremost a matter of students

empowering themselves to combat institutions that have frequently betrayed them, abandoned them, and sought to sweep
sexual assault allegations under the carpet. But by going public
with their stories, the young women and men of *The Hunting
Ground* have also begun to dispel the aura of doubt and shame
and secrecy that has often permitted onlookers to conclude *There
must be more here than meets the eye,* or *Well, she could be a jilted
lover,* or *He said, she said—what can we do?*

One of the hardest facts for men to absorb about rape is also
one of the simplest, and its difficulty comes from the fact that it
challenges deeply encoded male narratives about sexual consent
that most men do not discuss, and may not consciously recognize.
Rape allegations are not inherently different from other criminal
accusations: The vast majority of them are likely to be true.

That is not to say that accused rapists are not entitled to due
process, the presumption of innocence, and the right to defend
themselves, and no one has suggested otherwise. False accusations
or cases of mistaken identity can and do occur, as with any other
kind of crime. Every one of those that surfaces in the media, I am
sorry to say, is seized upon as evidence that women are hysterical
alien beings who fabricate vengeful fantasies and whose testimony
cannot be trusted.

But the overwhelming weight of the evidence—and the overwhelming weight of the strikingly similar narratives we hear in
the film—points in an entirely different direction. Most sexual
assault allegations are highly plausible, and not especially confus-
ing or unclear. Yet a vanishingly small number of them result in any
meaningful consequences for the accused perpetrator. For the male
viewer of *The Hunting Ground,* or at least for this one, it's impossible
to avoid the conclusion that we have failed the present college-age

generation. But they have not failed us: The young women (and men) who tell their stories in this film have given us an opportunity to face the reality of male denial, and to change it.

Andrew O'Hehir is a senior writer at Salon *covering culture and politics. He has written for the* New York Times, *the* Washington Post, *the* Times *(UK), and numerous other publications, and writes a monthly column on Hollywood for* Elle China. *He is the author of three plays and a forthcoming young-adult novel, and is at work on a family memoir about his parents and J. Edgar Hoover.*

School of Trauma

by D. Watkins

Samantha, who went by Sammy to most, but just Sam to me, lived down the block. She was lanky in foggy frames, knock-kneed, boyish, and liked to hoop with my friends and me even though she was a few years older than us. Sam wasn't really a ball player; she just liked to goof around, clown, critique us, and occasionally fill in when we needed an extra player.

I used to always say, "Sam, you gonna be my manager when I hit the league!" and everybody else followed suit as they should've— Sam was the smartest girl in our neighborhood, the kid who went to all types of science and debate camps, so no one was surprised when she got accepted into the University of Maryland.

Sam's mom and stepdad threw her a prom/getting into college cookout. Our whole block showed up, jamming the alley until it was standing room only. The party was live because the hood loved Sam and there weren't too many people going to college on our East Baltimore block. Plus her big brother Lil Jesse came home from prison. He sat three years because of a parole violation for having dirty piss or something.

Us kids shot hoops on the milk crate strapped to the phone pole in the midst of all the confusion. Old Head grilled beef franks and tiny turkey burgers while the rest of the adults two-stepped to Marvin Gaye, played dominos, and sipped warm yak. "Here she come, y'all!" Sam's mom yelled, clipping the music. "Ohhhhhhhh's," rang out as everyone gawked and pointed in her direction.

Sam inched out in a black gown, her hair was pinned away from her face—showing her sharp features, and she had on red lipstick—Sam was bad and we never knew! We started calling her model-status after that. She ditched the tomboy look, hung with us less, and clicked up with those prissy girls from up the street who only wore leggings.

The summer flashed past and the many yellows and oranges of fall crept in. We were all back in school and Sam was off to College Park. She rarely came home that first semester. I caught her over the break once. "The work is killing me. It's so hard to keep up!" Sam told me. "And the 10,000 weekly parties don't help. College Park is a party town!"

Sam grew up a lot in that first semester. She cut her hair short into one of those Halle Berry layered do's, she ditched all of her boy clothes for good, smoked weed like a Marley, and drank. "Everybody in college drinks," Sam told a pack of us under a streetlight one night. "That's mandatory at any college party!"

The next semester lasted about two weeks for Sam. Lil Jesse walked by my house with a low brawl and flared nostrils—leaped up my steps and thumped on my front door. "Is your brother in the house?" he asked without giving me time to answer, "Bip, I need you! Bip!" My older brother let him in. Lil Jesse yelled something like "bring 100 guns" and stormed back out. Bip called me in the house. "Yo, I gotta handle Sammy problem wit Lil Jesse," he said.

"Damn, is she okay?" I asked.

"Naw, bro. She was date-raped," Bip replied, wiping off his pistol and placing it in his waistline. My brother explained that date rape is when you start getting with a girl you know, who then changes her mind, but you force her to have sex anyway. "If a girl say no you gotta stop. You can go to jail for that shit!" Bip said, "Some college boy is about to get his head knocked off for that shit, it's wrong!"

Lil Jesse assembled a crew to hit the campus so they could find the culprit and beat him down. About 13 dudes packed up in a car and a MPV van—Sam was like everybody's sister, and that rapist wasn't going to get away, is what I thought.

But when they got to the campus, some dudes who knew my brother and Lil Jesse said her story was fake. "Hell nah, she didn't get raped," they told Lil Jesse. "She's a drunk party girl and that's how she get down!" Some other students, including women, confirmed that Sam's story wasn't true.

Lil Jesse and his mob left without harming anyone. Sam eventually dropped out of school to never return. She rarely talked about her brief college stint, and was never really the same afterward. She now roams the streets and chain-smokes with a nervous twitch. Her hair is thin and her face is worn beyond her years. I tried to spark up a convo with her once before, but it was awkward for the both of us.

Rape culture is as old as campus culture, and the rapist and rapist protectors seem to band together as much or even more than the victims. That same rape culture of entitlement, misogyny, and hyper-masculinity made Jesse side with those losers over his little sister. I wasn't there, but I knew Sam forever and she wouldn't make that up.

Writing, films like *The Hunting Ground*, and using art as a weapon of awareness are all powerful ways powerful way to get people's attention. But I think we also need to do what we can to suck the money from colleges and universities by constantly harassing their administrations, disrupting their major sporting events, and even refusing to enroll as long as they tolerate campus rape. Because there are millions of Sams out there who need our support.

D. Watkins is the author of The Beast Side: Living (and Dying) while Black in America, *and a columnist for* Salon. *His work has been published in the* New York Times, *the* Huffington Post, Aeon, AlterNet, The Guardian, *and other magazines. He is a frequent guest on NPR's Monday Morning,* Tell Me More, The Real News Network, Huff Post Live, *and* The Marc Steiner Show. *He teaches at Goucher University and has been the recipient of numerous awards including a BMe fellowship,* Baltimore Magazine's *"Best Writer" award for 2015, and* The Baltimore Business Journal's *"40 under 40" list. He holds a master's in education from Johns Hopkins University and an MFA in creative writing from the University of Baltimore. Watkins grew up and lives in East Baltimore.*

Sexual Assault and the Media

by Christina Asquith

The email threat was vicious and detailed: If I kept writing about sexual misconduct on college campuses, the email said, my family would be harmed. The anonymous author had created an email account in my father's name, and even listed my parents' home address.

Online harassment, trolling, and bullying are widespread, but they are particularly pronounced for female journalists. A report from the Columbia School of Journalism found that more than 60 percent of women journalists have experienced verbal sexual harassment, while the International Federation of Journalists concluded that the online targeting of women journalists had become so problematic that they have launched a global campaign to raise awareness of the issue.

Covering sexual assault makes journalists particularly vulnerable to attack, even when their reporting is straightforward and balanced. In my case, for example, I received threats after I made a comment in *The New York Times* challenging the notion of "rape hoax culture." (Some media outlets—Fox News, *Weekly Standard*, *National Review*,and *Slate* among them—have promoted the idea that a "rape hoax culture" exists on many college campuses, with young women rushing forward to submit false assault claims against innocent male students.)

The fact is that false rape reports make up only between 2 to 8 percent of total claims, which is the same rate of false reporting as most other crimes. Yet as reports of forcible sex offenses on college campuses have jumped 50 percent (from 2,500 to 3,900) between 2009 and 2012, more men are going public to challenge the accusations, and giving credence to the notion that rape victims frequently fabricate their stories.

Why do those who come forward to report rape, and the journalists who cover these incidents, face so much opposition? The answer to this question is complex and likely has to do, at least in part, with bias against women and societal taboos about rape—attitudes that seem to trigger a reflexive denial of the issue. These attitudes are so prevalent in our culture that it's no surprise that they are reflected in the media.

It isn't just right-wing bloggers who are denying reports of campus assault. Many reputable news organizations—in the name of balance—perpetuate the myth that women frequently lie about being raped, either by highlighting claims of false reporting, echoing charges of "rape hoax culture" without examining the research, or avoiding the topic altogether.

This widespread denial has far-reaching consequences. We know, for example, that only 18 percent of rape cases are prosecuted. These crimes can be hard to prove, but many cases aren't ever pursued. An exhaustive investigation by *USA Today,* for example, found that thousands of rape kits (forensic evidence taken after a woman has been assaulted) held at police stations around the country have never been tested. DNA testing of these kits could be used to find and charge the perpetrators.

The *USA Today* investigation, a 2015 *Washington Post* series on campus sexual assault, the film *The Hunting Ground*, and similar investigations are helping to raise awareness of the issue, but sloppy reporting can have the opposite effect. A prime example of this is the flawed 2014 *Rolling Stone* article asserting a vicious gang rape took place at the University of Virginia (UVA) and that administrators looked the other way.

The article, which was poorly sourced and inadequately fact-checked, was later retracted, and the editor forced to resign. The magazine now faces lawsuits from UVA and the fraternity implicated in the article. The incident unleashed a storm of media coverage focused on false reporting that far outweighed coverage of actual sexual assaults. By focusing primarily on media scandal and "rape hoax," the issue of colleges covering up sexual assaults was overlooked. In fact, few commentators even mentioned that while UVA has expelled 183 people for cheating on tests or similar honor code violations since 1998, it has never expelled a single student for sexual assault. Instead, many journalists and pundits have pounced on the article as evidence that false reporting is common and that the issue of campus assault is overblown. Fox News host Andrea Tantaros declared after the *Rolling Stone* incident, "There is a war happening. On boys. On these college campuses."

A study by the group Media Matters, for example, found that two-thirds of cable news shows only covered the issue of gang rapes on college campuses after *Rolling Stone* made its retraction.

"Why is there more interest in *Rolling Stone*'s screw-up than in the toxic mix of entitlement, alcohol, and zero accountability that have led to one in five women being raped during her college years?" asked Krystal Ball, an MSNBC reporter who has reported on the imbalance in coverage.

News editors insist they have not shied away from pursuing articles on sexual violence since the *Rolling Stone* debacle. But anti-rape advocacy organizations have seen a drop in coverage post–*Rolling Stone*. According to Laura Dunn, an attorney and founder of SurvJustice, "It went from three calls a day to maybe three calls a week. We are seeing a big downturn, less interest in covering it," Dunn told Media Matters.

Other news organizations are treading cautiously, when they cover the issue at all. Jenny Wilkinson, who wrote about being raped at the University of Virginia in a 2015 *New York Times* op-ed, was required by the *Times* to include a rebuttal by her assailant in her column. (He was found guilty for the assault; his only sanction was a letter in his file.) This type of point-counterpoint is rarely demanded of other op-ed contributors on pages that are filled with personal opinions and narratives, many of them highlighting injustices.

Several writer colleagues have told me that editors are finding excuses not to cover assault stories. Just recently, for example, two editors rejected a colleague's pitch for an article on marital rape. Both told her they wouldn't publish anything on rape unless the reporter contacted the accused, which often makes such stories impossible, because women who have been assaulted don't want to contact their aggressors, and aggressors are unlikely to cooperate with a reporter.

Of course, reporters should apply skepticism to all sides of the stories they report, and rigorously pursue the facts wherever they lead. But if the media focuses primarily on rape hoax stories, or presents assaults as strictly "he said, she said" incidents, or avoids the issue altogether, it will be a victory for those who insist that campus sexual violence is a matter of rare, isolated incidents, and not a systemic problem. Filmmakers like Kirby Dick and Amy Ziering prove that strong, enterprising coverage of sexual assault can shed valuable light on an issue that for too long has dwelled in the shadows of misconception and denial.

Christina Asquith is founder of The Fuller Project for International Reporting @FPIR. A journalist for 20 years, she is author of Sisters in War: The Story of Love, Family and Survival in the New Iraq.

Sports on Trial

by Jessica Luther

In *The Hunting Ground*, Annie Clark recounts what an administrator at the University of North Carolina told her when she reported her assault: "Rape is like a football game, Annie, and if you look back on the game, what would you do differently in that situation?" The quote is jarring because of course it's not Clark but her rapist who should have made a different choice. It's also a good narrative device because the way universities protect athletes—especially football players—who have been accused of sexual assault is a major focus of the film.

Rape is not, in fact, like a football game. But too often we find ourselves talking about campus sexual assault because a football player or other high-profile athlete has been accused. As a journalist who writes almost exclusively about sports, I've come to the conclusion that there's no way to tell the full story of campus sexual assault without addressing its intersection with college sports.

It isn't clear that athletes actually commit more sexual assault than non-athlete undergraduates (though some studies have suggested this and *The Hunting Ground* cites figures from one of these studies). We tend to hear more about attacks by athletes because when it comes to news about colleges and universities, sports media is the most dedicated and far-reaching. College sports is a billion-dollar business, and colleges pour tremendous resources into their sports programs. In addition, sports is the lens through which most people connect to their alma maters and learn about what is happening there. College athletic fans are deeply invested, both emotionally and financially, in these young men and their sports teams.

Athletes, in other words, receive more attention than non-athlete students, which means that when when a student athlete is accused of sexual assault, the incident tends to receive more coverage. But all this attention is part of the problem. Even if they don't commit *more* assaults, they commit a good share, and the culture of entitlement that surrounds these athletes means that, in many cases, their position as a member of the team carries more weight than the crime or its victim. As Abby Ross, one young woman interviewed for *The Hunting Ground*, put it: "I felt like because he [her assailant] was an athlete everyone was acting like he's worth more than I am."

This special treatment can be intoxicating for student athletes, who are still teenagers when they enter college. Compared to the average Joe student, these young men and women are a big deal: Their faces are well-known around campus, and their team and its successes are celebrated at school and in the surrounding community. They're profiled in the media; they are put in front of microphones and cameras and asked their opinions on a variety of subjects; some players wind up on the covers of national magazines.

The special attention starts early—as does the message that becoming a college athlete confers rarified, celebrity status. When some schools recruit athletes, for example—particularly those with profit-producing teams in high-profile programs—they send the athlete a Photoshopped image of himself walking arm-in-arm with a beautiful female celebrity—an implicit promise of the future if they sign with that school (and a not-so-subtle message that access to women is a reward for sports stardom).

If a student athlete is accused of an assault, his status as a player on a prized team means that the college system has a stake in protecting him from the negative consequences of that behavior. A 2014 report by Senator Claire McCaskill revealed that protection of athletes is built into the system at many colleges: At 22 percent of the institutions surveyed, athletic departments had oversight over sexual assault allegations made against athletes, an approach that McCaskill called "borderline outrageous."

In *The Hunting Ground*, retired Notre Dame police officer Pat Cottrell told filmmakers that college administrators there forbid campus police from contacting athletes at practice or at their campus housing—even those suspected of infractions. (Cottrell quit his job after Notre Dame refused to pursue an athlete accused of sexually assaulting a student from St. Mary's, Notre Dame's sister school.)

Cottrell's experience shouldn't come as a surprise, given what we've learned over the years about the seamy underside of college sports. Barry Switzer, who was head football coach at the University of Oklahoma in the Seventies and Eighties, and earned one of the highest winning records of any college coach in history, later admitted that his players got special treatment from local law enforcement. "I'd have local county people call me and say, 'One of your guys is drunk and got in a fight and is in jail down here,'" Switzer said. "I'd go down and get him out. Or I'd send an assistant coach down to get his ass out. The sheriff was a friend of the program. He didn't want the publicity. He himself knew this was something we didn't need to deal with in the media. Most coaches ran it that way. We all did."

Last year, the *New York Times* reported on the cozy relationship between Florida State University's athletic department and Tallahassee police: "In a community whose self-image and economic well-being are so tightly bound to the fortunes of the nation's top-ranked college football team, law enforcement officers are finely attuned to a suspect's football connections. Those ties are cited repeatedly in police reports examined by the *Times*. What's more, dozens of officers work second jobs directing traffic and providing security at home football games, and many express their devotion to the Seminoles on social media."

In my own reporting, I've found that many women don't want to report an athlete because they know that they will be the one to land under the hostile bright lights of public scrutiny if their favorite player loses time on the field. That was certainly the case for Erica Kinsman, the Florida State University student who accused quarterback Jameis Winston of raping her. Kinsman told *The Hunting Ground* filmmakers that she was warned by the Tallahassee police detective in charge of the investigation, an FSU alum himself, "This is a huge football town. You really should think long and hard about whether you want to press charges or not." In the film, FSU fans deride Kinsman, while one refers rapturously to Winston as "Jameis Christ." Both Kinsman's family and sorority received threats after she reported the alleged assault. She ultimately dropped out of FSU, while Winston, who won the Heisman trophy, is now playing for the NFL.

While I was writing this piece, I was also working on an article about a Baylor University football player who was being tried for sexual assault (he's since been convicted) and monitoring news about a retrial for two Vanderbilt football players convicted of the crime. In the three years I've been covering college sports, I have heard of and/or reported on more than twenty-five incidents of allegations or charges of sexual assault by college football players.

It's discouraging that these incidents keep happening, but I am hopeful that their increased visibility signals a shift in societal attitudes toward and tolerance of these crimes. As *The Hunting Ground* points out, a growing number of campus activists are demanding reform of campus anti-sexual assault policies—and for changes in campus culture as a whole.

Given their high-profile status, college athletes could play an important role in the transformation of campus culture. But this won't happen unless coaches and college leaders demand more of athletes by making it clear that sexual violence and harassment are unacceptable. Some college coaches understand this and are setting a positive example. University of Texas coach Charlie Strong, for example, suspended two of his players after they were charged with assaulting a student." It's been made clear to everyone on our team that treating women with respect is one of our core values, and I'm extremely disappointed that two young men in our program have been accused of not doing that," Strong said in a public statement. Strong maintained a similar player code of conduct at his previous post as coach at the University of Louisville.

This is good, but it is the minimum of what athletic departments could be doing. Instead of waiting for violence to happen, some teams are incorporating anti–sexual assault education into their sports curriculum.

We will continue to see a link between sports and sexual assault until college administrators, athletic departments, coaches, and teammates hold athletes accountable, while also finally teaching these players about consent, and about the worth and humanity of women.

Jessica Luther is a freelance journalist living in Austin, Texas. Her writing has appeared in Sports Illustrated, Texas Monthly, Vice Sports, Bleacher Report, *the* Texas Observer, *and the* Austin Chronicle. *Her first book,* Unsportsmanlike Conduct: College Football and the Politics of Rape, *will be published later this year by Akashic Books.*

Faculty and the Campus Anti-Rape Movement

by Alissa R. Ackerman and Caroline Heldman

*T*he *Hunting Ground* touches only briefly on the role of university faculty in the campus anti-rape movement. Behind most survivors who speak out is a faculty member encouraging them, and many faculty members have faced retaliation for their voices and their support. Still, as faculty members ourselves, we believe that university faculty are in a unique position to support survivors and help create more effective campus anti-rape policies—and that doing so will benefit students and institutions alike.

Research shows that nearly one in five women and 6 percent of men will experience sexual assault during college. Despite its prevalence on campuses around the country, most faculty consider sexual violence an administrative problem, or an issue that has little do with a student's academic life. In our experience, this is a mistake and a missed opportunity.

Ken Schneck, a professor at Baldwin Wallace University, pointed out in *The Huffington Post* that students do not simply leave the issue of sexual assault outside of the classroom. Faculty have frequent contact with students, and when they pay attention, they can spot signs of trauma—from decreased work quality to sudden classroom withdrawal. In many cases, far from their parents and family, a student who experiences a sexual attack often confides in a professor she or he trusts. Their position on the front lines of campus life represents a tremendous opportunity for faculty to help individual sexual assault survivors, and to foster long-term change in campus culture.

While the majority of faculty have remained silent on sexual assault issues, a few are experts on the topic and advocate for student survivors. The campus anti-rape movement is an informal network of student survivors, professors, and anti-violence activists outside the academy. It is more than 40 years in the making, and a small but active number of faculty have been involved in the movement from its inception. Faculty have developed and hosted anti-sexual violence programs on campus for almost four decades, such as Take Back the Night, Sexual Assault Awareness Week, The Clothesline Project, and *The Vagina Monologues*.

In 2013, amidst a flurry of new activity and awareness of campus sexual assault, the new campus anti-rape movement was born. It includes students, alumni, faculty, and a few administrators. According to campus safety activist S. Daniel Carter, the new movement has been extremely successful and has helped position campus sexual violence as a national policy issue—one that has finally captured public attention

Shamed, Silenced, Terminated

The Hunting Ground includes interviews with professors who helped assault survivors, or pushed for change in campus policies—and then found themselves out of a job. They are not alone. College administrators, concerned that potential students and their parents will be scared off by reports of sexual assaults, too often ignore or minimize sexual assault incidents, and push back against the efforts of faculty activists with silencing tactics and retaliation. This led the U.S. Department of Education to warn college administrators against retaliation in 2013, but despite this warning, many faculty still experience negative consequences for their work on sexual violence issues.

Retaliation may include inconvenient teaching schedules, denial of research funding and leave requests, and the re-allocation of resources away from an entire department that employ an anti-assault activist. All of the faculty we have worked with through the organizations End Rape on Campus (EROC) and Faculty Against Rape (FAR) have experienced negative changes in the way they are treated by their institution after speaking out about sexual assault.

Faculty who speak out do so knowing that it can fundamentally and inevitably change their career trajectories. For example, Jennifer Freyd, one of the most influential experts on institutional betrayal and campus sexual assault in the world, faced denial of research requests on campus climate at the University of Oregon. The president of Occidental College, Jonathan Veitch, chastised a faculty member in a public statement for embarrassing the college after she spoke out about Occidental's problems with campus sexual assault. Several untenured faculty (who requested anonymity) have been publicly shamed by senior faculty, both to students and other faculty, by suggesting that their research on sexual violence or their support of survivors could not be trusted because of their poor mental or emotional states.

Underrepresented faculty, including women in general, women of color, and queer individuals, are at particular risk of retaliation given their already precarious position in the academy. They are in less secure positions when it comes to tenure and promotion to begin with, so speaking out about sexual violence on campus may put their professional life in jeopardy. One queer faculty member (who requested anonymity) was targeted by another faculty member as mentally unstable after speaking out in support of survivors on her campus.

Some, like the professors who appear in *The Hunting Ground*, face employment retaliation. Kimberly Theidon, a former professor of anthropology at Harvard with an impressive research and teaching record, was denied tenure after speaking out about victim-blaming. Political science professor Heather Turcotte had her contract terminated after criticizing the president of the University of Connecticut for her response to students filing sexual assault complaints. Other faculty around the country have had their promotions delayed, their tenure denied, or their contracts terminated for speaking out.

Faculty Against Rape

Despite this chilling climate, a small number of faculty play key roles in the anti-rape movement at a number of different levels. Faculty research on campus sexual assault has provided the data on which the campus anti-violence movement relies. The first study on campus sexual assault dates back to the 1950s, and several landmark studies have been published since. Mary Koss is known for her seminal 1982 work showing that most rape and sexual assault is committed by acquaintances. Peggy Sanday's book *Fraternity Gang Rape* explores the cultural aspects of fraternities that promote rape and rape culture. Today, faculty research has played a key role in highlighting that sexual violence is endemic to university life.

Another way faculty help combat campus sexual assault is teaching courses that address it. Based on a sample of course catalogs of four-year institutions in the U.S., we estimate that more than 10,000 courses are taught each year that formally include sexual violence as a topic. For many students, these courses offer an opportunity to put their experience of sexual assault into words and context for the first time. These courses propel other students into anti–sexual assault activism.

Meanwhile, a handful of faculty activists have played essential roles in the campus anti–sexual violence movement from the beginning. The new movement gained momentum in 2013 after a decade of legal work initiated by faculty. In fact, since 2013 more than 100 Title IX investigations have been opened by the Department of Education concerning issues of college sexual assault because of the legal work initiated by faculty in the early 2000s.

After high-profile Title IX cases at Harvard and Yale that were initiated by student survivors with the help of professor Diane Rosenfeld, the Education Department issued a Dear Colleague Letter with new guidelines for how the law should be applied to campus sexual violence.

Faculty activists have helped file federal complaints and created national organizations to address both campus sexual assault and faculty involvement in the movement. Professor Wendy Murphy, for example, filed a Title IX complaint against Harvard in 2002, and later founded the organization Campus Accountability. In 2013, after filing Title IX and Clery complaints against Occidental College, professors Caroline Heldman, Danielle Dirks, and several students cofounded EROC, an organization that has assisted activists from dozens of other schools file Title IX complaints. The organization One in Four was formed by Professor John Foubert at Oklahoma State University. Faculty Against Rape was the first faculty organization formed to address campus sexual violence. It was cofounded by Bill Flack (Bucknell University), Simona Sharoni (SUNY Plattsburgh), and Caroline Heldman (Occidental College). Since its inception in 2014, FAR has assisted faculty at over 200 institutions.

Despite almost assured institutional retaliation, a growing number of faculty are speaking out about sexual assault on their campuses. As the only constituency on campus long-term (compared to students and administrators who spend an average of four and five years on campus, respectively), their participation can have a lasting impact on institutional reform. It is essential for more faculty to add their voices to the campus anti-rape movement. The more faculty who do so, the less retaliation individual faculty will face.

Dr. Alissa R. Ackerman is assistant professor of criminal justice in the Social Work Program at the University of Washington, Tacoma. She has almost a decade of experience studying the nature, context, and extent of sexual victimization, and has written extensively on policy and practice related to individuals who commit sex crimes. Her book, Sex Crimes: Transnational Problems and Global Perspectives, *was recently published by Columbia University Press.*

Dr. Caroline Heldman is an associate professor of politics at Occidental College in Los Angeles. Her research specializes in the presidency, systems of power (race, class, gender, and sexuality), and sexual violence. Her work has been featured in the top journals in her field; she co-edited Rethinking Madam President: Are We Ready for a Woman in the White House? *(2007). Dr. Heldman has been active in "real world" politics as a professional pollster, campaign manager, and commentator for MSNBC, FOX News, Fox Business News, CNBC, and Al Jazeera America. She splits her time between Los Angeles and New Orleans, where she cofounded the New Orleans Women's Shelter and the Lower Ninth Ward Living Museum. Dr. Heldman also cofounded End Rape on Campus (EROC) and Faculty Against Rape (FAR).*

Familiar Territory

by Erin Ryan

The calls would come at different times of day, but the sound at the other end of the line was always the same. I'd pick up. There would be a pause, then a light, shuddering breath.

Through tears, she'd explain what had just happened to her a day, a week, a month ago. My friend—a different one each time—had been sexually assaulted.

The friend on the other end of the phone wouldn't call it "rape"; she'd flip and spin around the word, calling it "passed-out sex," or "he kind of roughly decided we were going to have sex," or "he sat on my chest and I couldn't move my arms sex," without landing on the act's simple ugliness. But in every one of the incidents my friends endured during our time in college, that's what it was. None of them reported what happened to them to anyone in a position of authority. What would be the point? My friends who were raped in college knew that working their way through our university's disciplinary Rube Goldberg machine would result in social ostracization and a long, drawn-out bureaucratic process as terrible in its own way as the violation they'd already endured.

My college, the University of Notre Dame, and its sister school, the all-women Saint Mary's College, as Catholic institutions, have a built-in and archaic shame-based view of sexuality. Rules layered on top of that foundation added even more stigma and confusion to the subject of sex. During my tenure there from 2001 to 2005, being caught having consensual sex was grounds for disciplinary action up to and including dismissal. Students were also subjected to strict visiting hours in their exclusively single-sex dorms. To want sex was shameful, but to have your parents find out that you'd been suspended for a semester for being with a boy outside of visiting hours was even more shameful. And until recently, embarrassingly, it wasn't clear in the student handbook that a woman who reported being raped by a male student outside of designated visiting hours wouldn't be disciplined herself for breaking the rules.

The stories of the women in *The Hunting Ground* are similar to my friends' tearful confessions of a decade ago, and women I interviewed for articles a year ago, a month ago (in fact, I was once on an Al Jazeera America panel on sexual assault with Andrea Pino and Annie E. Clark, student activists featured prominently in *The Hunting Ground*). The shuddering breaths are the same. The fear of taking on a powerful and entitled athlete at an elite school is the same. The tears and smudged mascara are the same. Even the landscape is familiar: I walked to liturgical choir practice on one of the paths featured in B-roll footage of the campus.

Viewers will undoubtedly describe *The Hunting Ground* with all manner of pull quote–ready phrases. A male acquaintance called the film a "gut-punch." To a layperson who hasn't spent more than a decade reading, writing, and listening to stories about sexual assault, the film will present new information and humanize a heated and emotional issue. But for me the most disturbing element of the film was how truly unsurprised I was by every single element of it. It was like seeing dozens of conversations I'd had with women (and a few men) played extra-large on the big screen.

Since residential post-secondary education has existed as a rite of passage for a large chunk of middle- and upper-class American teenagers, predatory students have targeted vulnerable classmates. Colleges have always been ridiculously ill-equipped to effectively address sexual assault. The difference between what's going on today and those hushed phone calls 10 years ago is that college students now feel empowered to talk to somebody besides their friends about being sexually assaulted. Instead of internalizing the shame of date rape, they understand that sex without consent isn't sex at all. They know that when their university fails to protect them, they can do something about it.

Erin Ryan is the managing editor of Jezebel, *where she covers politics, current events, and culture. She was born in Wisconsin and currently resides in Brooklyn.*

The Ambitious Storytelling of *The Hunting Ground*

by Wendy Levy

"... I believed myself to be banging on the door of History, demanding that my memories be let in."

—Tayari Jones

There is nothing easy about *The Hunting Ground*. It is a movie that enters your consciousness and doesn't leave. It is a work of documentary art where the voices of survivors of sexual assault on American college campuses drive a dogged and dramatic narrative. From the first frame to the very last, this explosive story of broken dreams, violated bodies, and corrupt systems requires our unbroken attention.

To understand how a film like *The Hunting Ground* works, I did some research on Kirby Dick and Amy Ziering's body of work, and I came across some words of Jacques Derrida, the French philosopher who was the focus of the first film Dick and Ziering worked on together (*Derrida*, 2002) that resonated for me:

"If this work seems so threatening, this is because it isn't simply eccentric or strange . . . but competent, rigorously argued, and carrying conviction."

The Hunting Ground is even more than a competent work of rigorous conviction. It is more than a contribution to the misinterpreted tradition of "advocacy documentary," where films about urgent social issues have been trapped in a conundrum of

113

perception somewhere among strategic communications, issue-based marketing, and actual works of art. While Ford Foundation's JustFilms director Cara Mertes speaks of the false dichotomy between art and social issues, Sundance Institute Documentary Film Program head Tabitha Jackson emphasizes that "the lingua franca of nonfiction filmmaking should be the language of cinema, not grant applications."

In recent years, a number of ambitious documentaries have side-stepped this conundrum to tell stories that have resonated far beyond their target audiences. These filmmakers understand the power of their medium; they also understand that before a culture changes, new stories must take root. The BRITDOC Foundation, a UK-based nonprofit that supports and promotes documentary filmmaking, highlights some of these transformative films in case studies on its website.

In *Granito*, for example, a documentary that is part memoir and part political thriller, director Pamela Yates describes how her 1983 documentary, *When the Mountains Tremble*, provided evidence that ultimately indicted Guatemalan dictator Rios Montt for crimes against humanity for his war against the Maya people.

In her film *Budrus*, director Julia Bachafocuses on Palestinian community organizer, Ayed Morrar, who unites Palestinian political factions and invites Israeli supporters to join an unarmed movement to save his village from destruction. The multi-year campaign that accompanied the film brought together a host of unlikely allies to change the global conversation about nonviolence. The film is about one Palestinian village, but it tells a much bigger story about what is possible in the Middle East.

In the 2013 film *Blackfish*, Gabriela Cowperthwaite told the brutal story of orca whales in captivity at SeaWorld and other marine parks, and triggered a powerful and widespread public reaction dubbed the "Blackfish effect": corporate sponsors pulled out of SeaWorld, the number of visitors plummeted, and profits dropped 84 percent after the film's release.

And *Bully*, a wrenching and controversial film by Lee Hirsch about bullying and its effects on children, was launched in tandem with "The Bully Project," a creative and educational engagement campaign designed to spark a national movement to end bullying. The project's initial goal was to reach one million kids; to date, 3.6 million kids have seen the film.

Beyond their deliberate vision to change a piece of the world, Kirby Dick and Amy Ziering say they also believe that "one of the most significant characteristics of artists is ambition—and their responsibility is to take on as much as possible." For them, the dichotomy between art and change is nonexistent. Their film *The Invisible War* exposed sexual assault in the military and triggered policy change at the national level. After a series of strategic Capitol Hill screenings, Leon Panetta, then Secretary of Defense, announced substantial changes in the way the military prosecutes sexual violence. With *The Hunting Ground*, the filmmakers are launching an equally strategic strategic effort to get word out about campus sexual assault and create national policy shifts. They have flown around the country to screen the film on numerous college campuses. They've reached out to legislators, and shown the documentary at the White House. They kicked off an ambitious social media campaign. A shorter version of the film for high school students is in the works. Beyond screenings, the website enables people to get involved in their communities, and offers specific and targeted resources for students, parents, college administrators, faculty, and the general public.

The power of *The Hunting Ground* lies not only in the campaign designed to get its message out, but in the film's capacity to *be* the change itself. Each public screening of *The Hunting Ground* can be seen as a transformative cultural experience where victims, by sharing their stories, become survivors; and we, as a society, move one step closer to empathy and equality.

When we talk about documentary film in the digital age, the unprecedented power of the web to connect people and movements underscores the potential of film to influence social change more than ever before. Some artists love the challenge and fully embrace it; others push back as if you've asked them to cut off their right arm. There is an indescribable impact when artists make a claim to find the unique creative gestures that lead audiences beyond the screen—into the streets, the university offices, the voting booths, and the halls of power. As both artists and activists, Amy Ziering and Kirby Dick have inspired a new generation of filmmakers and journalists to imagine a world where the end of their story is not the end of *the* story.

Wendy Levy works with communities around the world at the intersection of art, innovation, and social change. She is the executive director of the National Alliance for Media Arts and Culture and a senior consultant with the Sundance Institute Documentary Film Program. Wendy is the recipient of the Princess Grace Statue Award for distinguished contribution to the media arts field, and lives in Oakland, California.

Target Rape on Campus

by Diane Rosenfeld

The documentary film *The Hunting Ground* exposes the systemic problem of campus sexual assault. Through harrowing narratives of student–survivors, we see the profoundly devastating effects that one act of sexual violence can have on a victim's entire educational trajectory. Rape is all too prevalent on college campuses and represents a massive deprivation of women's civil rights to educational equality.

The narratives in the film expose a pattern of behavior I refer to as "target rape." In contrast to the stereotype of rape as an act committed by a dangerous stranger, target rape describes a situation in which men, often with support from their male social group, intentionally incapacitate women through the use of drugs or alcohol and have sex with them. Target rapists do this knowing that a victim's incapacitated condition may enable them to camouflage the rape as a drunken hookup or regretted sex. Humor and "fun, drunken, irresponsible" college behavior cloaks—or tries to cloak—the sexual dominance men are asserting, creating an environment of rape-supportive attitudes.[1]

When an individual declares his intention to "go out and get laid tonight, no matter what," this may be a precursor to target rape. His victim may not be a date, or even an acquaintance, but more likely someone he meets that night. He might incapacitate her through drugs or alcohol (or both) to make her more vulnerable.[2] The concept of target rape builds on the work of Dr. David Lisak, whose research into "undetected rapists" indicates that students who commit campus rape act in intentional, premeditated, and predatory ways.[3]

The term "target rape" shifts the focus of the behavior to the perpetrator's actions and away from the victim–offender relationship. It replaces "acquaintance" or "date" rape, which seem to blind us to our ability to judge a case, believing that a "he said, she said" credibility contest is unresolvable. It helps us move past the victim blaming frame in which we question the woman's behavior rather than focus on the person committing the assault. Rape shouldn't be a risk of socializing or partying with other students from your school. The worst thing that should happen to a young woman who parties at school is that she wakes up with a hangover.

Those who argue that sexual assault cases involving college students should simply be handled by the criminal justice system are missing the critical point that schools have legal obligations to enforce the civil rights of students. Title IX protects the rights of students to equal access to educational opportunities. Sexual harassment, of which sexual assault is an extreme form, can create a hostile environment at school and deprive a student of her or his rights. *The Hunting Ground* attests to the alarming prevalence of precisely this deprivation. A recent study conducted by the American Association of Universities confirms the staggering statistics: 25 to 30 percent of female undergraduates surveyed had experienced nonconsensual sexual conduct involving force or incapacitation. If we do not act, hundreds of thousands of additional young women will be sexually assaulted at college this year.

Target rape describes cases in which males ally together in sexual pursuit of females not only regardless of the female's sexual desire, but often in deliberate violation of it. Male-only exclusive spaces, such as fraternities or athletic teams, often serve as breeding grounds for the transmission of misogynistic attitudes that contribute to a sexual culture on campus that devalues women.

We know from reading the news how often fraternities are implicated in target rapes. And a look into fraternity social culture reveals attitudes that treat women as sexual objects for conquest rather than human beings.[4] For example, a fraternity brother at the University of Southern California published a weekly "Gullet Report" in which he described different names for different targets, explaining his reference to females *as targets*: "[t]hey aren't actual people like us men."[5]

While gang rape may be one of a woman's greatest fears, some fraternity members act as though it is a harmless bonding activity. Studies on masculinity indicate that gang rape, from the perspective of perpetrators, typically has more to do with cementing a bond between men than with the (often incapacitated) woman being raped.[6] The voyeurism evident in these cases is an important dimension of the assertion of male dominance in a gang rape, yet it is underanalyzed in the literature.[7] Cases of a single fraternity member raping an incapacitated woman often occur in rooms where other brothers can watch, and frat houses and other exclusive male clubs designate rooms for this purpose.[8]

The culture surrounding football teams seems to foster this behavior particularly often.[9,10] Such assaults often appear to reflect alliances among many players—generally implicit (but sometimes explicit) agreements to commit the assault, to cover it up, or to keep it from hurting the season.[11] Coaches, college administrators, and even prosecutors sometimes participate in these alliances.[12] A recent example is the rape case at Florida State University (FSU), in which a female student, Erica Kinsman, reported being raped after being given a drink at a bar that rendered her incapacitated.[13] She did not know her assailant's name when she went to the hospital for a rape kit just hours after the assault, but did recall an encounter with an FSU football player at the bar prior to the assault.[14] Kinsman alleges that even though she reported the name of the suspect—Jameis Winston—when she learned of it a few weeks later, FSU failed even to question him until after the football season had ended and he had led the team to win the college football national championship (see Chapter 2).[15] The male prosecutor who dropped the criminal charges actually laughed during a press conference about the case.[16] Another example involved three basketball players recently suspended from the University of Oregon for gang rape.[17] One of the players, Brandon Austin, had previously been suspended from the Providence College basketball team for sexually assaulting a female student with another player, who had also been suspended.[18] Austin had transferred to University of Oregon while on suspension.[19] One of the biggest Title IX football cases involved University of Colorado-Boulder (CU-Boulder) players and recruits accused of raping two young women. Lisa Simpson alleged that football players arranged for recruits to gang rape her and her roommate after they had gone to bed after a party.[20] The university settled the case for $2.85 million.[21] A number of officials from CU resigned or were fired amidst the controversy, including the college president and the football coach.[22]

The Supreme Court has recognized that exactly this type of target rape is evidence of gender-based animus. In *United States v. Morrison*,[23] the late Chief Justice Rehnquist wrote for the Court that if plaintiff Christy Brzonkala's allegations of rape were true, "no civilized system of justice could fail to provide her a remedy for the conduct of respondent Morrison."[24] In that case, the Court struck down the civil rights remedy of the Violence Against

Women Act, but implied there should have been a remedy for the assault claimed in the case.[25] Brzonkala's case has enormous significance here, as it is a clear example of target rape and of the male alliances among football players that insulated the players from being held responsible.[26] In brief, she alleged that she was raped by two football players, Antonio Morrison and James Crawford, within half an hour of meeting them.[27] She alleged that the rapes were committed early in her freshman year at Virginia Polytechnic Institute.[28] She also claimed that immediately following the rape, Morrison stated, "You better not have any . . . diseases."[29] Several months later, Morrison was overheard in the cafeteria making "boasting, debased remarks about what [he] would do to women."[30] All courts that heard the case considered this to be evidence of gender-based animus.[31]

The school initially suspended Morrison for a year after a hearing.[32] Crawford was not held responsible, at least in part because another football player, Cornell Brown, testified that Crawford was with him at the time of the rape.[33] However, Brown was also added to Brzonkala's complaint for aiding and abetting the other two players[34] by guarding the door of her dorm room.[35] Unbelievably, Virginia Tech overturned Morrison's sanction in an appeal of which Brzonkala was not informed, and suspended his suspension until he graduated.[36] Brzonkala alleged that the football coach, Frank Beamer, inappropriately intervened in the process to protect the player's ability to stay on the team.[37] Morrison returned to Virginia Tech on a full athletic scholarship.[38] Brzonkala was unable to continue her education at Virginia Tech and withdrew.[39]

This problem is cultural, in that these men are not taught that targeting women is not an acceptable social practice and can be a precursor to rape. Schools must recognize that language such as that used in the "Gullet Report" is not merely bantering between friends, but rather that it evinces a sexually hostile environment and publicly warns of potential rapes. Such language and behavior signal that problematic norms exist either within a particular group or on campus more broadly, and should prompt the school to address this targeting, rape-supportive behavior immediately.

The courage of a growing number of victims to disclose their sexual assaults, combined with the recent increase in the pressure brought to bear on colleges by the Department of Education,[40] has prompted many college administrators to initiate reforms of their institutions' sexual assault policies. Unfortunately, too often those reforms have been limited to adjustment of the rules governing the initiation and resolution of complaints. Those rules matter, of course. But transforming the environments that stunt the education of so many women requires much more.

So what are we to do? Schools have a threefold obligation under Title IX to prevent and address campus sexual assault, and within this obligation comes our answer. The requirements of preventive education, a trauma-informed response, and a prompt and equitable resolution of a case are the essential components of an effective approach to sexual violence at school.

While schools might not be able to prevent all rapes through strong preventive education and bystander intervention, they can and must prevent all "second rapes."[41] Countless survivors have described the institutional betrayal they experienced by their schools as comparable and sometimes even worse than the initial assault. A school's indifference or botched response to a student reporting rape can derail the victim's entire educational path, compromising their future economic opportunities. But schools can offer academic accommodations to help a student retain an educational foothold and prevent a downward spiral. Schools can learn from the film *The Hunting Ground* how to listen to survivors and respond in a compassionate way.

Finally, schools must hold perpetrators accountable in order to protect all students and to send the message that such behavior is not tolerated within their campus community. If a student found responsible for sexually assaulting another student is allowed to remain on campus, it can create a hostile environment for the student who has been violated and may put others at risk for future assaults.

The Hunting Ground has broken the long silence of rape survivors on campus by connecting the dots of systematic denial of the problem. And although the courageous survivor–activists who are leading this movement endured extremely painful experiences both in the assaults and the subsequent betrayal by their schools, the takeaway from the film is a message of hope. Our country is witnessing a transformative moment in how we address campus sexual assault. Let's not keep defending practices that silence survivors at the precise moment they are finding their voice. Let's instead keep focused on how much we can change the culture that supports this damaging and predatory behavior and envision a new one of sexual respect and mutuality.

Diane L. Rosenfeld is a leading national legal expert on Title IX and campus sexual assault. Ms. Rosenfeld is a lecturer on law and the founder and director of the Gender Violence Program at Harvard Law School. Prior to teaching at Harvard, she served as the senior counsel to the Office on Violence Against Women at the US Department of Justice.

Facing Each Other

by Lisa C. Knisely

In 2002, I completed my senior undergraduate research project at a small liberal arts college in the Midwest. The project, which I conducted with another woman, was about sexual assault on my college campus and the administrative response—or rather lack of response. We conducted focus groups with survivors on campus, administered a campus-wide survey, and made recommendations for policy change to the administration and the student government. We taped our mouths shut and showed up at a football game to protest the silencing of survivors. We met with Greek leadership to talk about sexism and homophobia in their chapters. I left college both proud and disillusioned by my experiences. Change seemed achingly slow and those in power on campus seemed to not really care about the issue.

Almost a decade later, I returned to my alma mater as a visiting lecturer while I was finishing my PhD in women's, gender, and sexuality studies. I found that the students were still organizing around the issue of sexual assault on campus. Sexual assaults were still happening and the administration was still handling these events primarily as a legal and public relations issue. So it didn't surprise me when, in 2014, the college was on the list of those being investigated by the federal government for violation of Title IX.

This "victory" seemed hollow to me. After watching the film *The Hunting Ground*, I began to understand why. The film's portrayal of sexual assault on college campuses and the way institutions respond did not surprise me. What stood out to me was the way

Andrea Pino and Annie Clark developed a network for responding to assault survivors outside of the university structure, and could therefore be responsive in all the ways that college administrators are not. That various educational institutions were being brought to justice became less important to me than the work Pino and Clark were doing to simply show up for survivors. This is most poignantly highlighted during a scene when the two women are in the car driving to see yet another survivor of sexual assault and Pino says, "It's the only way I get up in the morning. I would have given anything to have had someone who believed me, someone who supported me."

Some very brief and rudimentary remarks about feminist theory are in order here. A few feminist political theorists have been articulating for some time their reservations about turning to the state for protection. Carole Pateman, in her 1988 book, *The Sexual Contract,* argues that the social contract, the foundational idea upon which Western liberal democracies are based, was actually founded on the exclusion of women, thus effectively rendering them outside the protection of the law. Following Pateman, there has been a chorus of feminist scholars who are skeptical about feminists turning to the state to try to fix social inequality, perhaps especially where violence and sexual violence are concerned.

There is good practical and theoretical evidence that appealing to the state for help frequently further subordinates sexual assault survivors rather than effectively responding to the harm done to them. As such, feminists have had rigorous debates about how to organize political power in ways not dependent on the state for justice. One of the key insights of feminist scholarship in the last thirty years is the recognition that the state is reliant on the subordination of its citizens for its very power. In return, the state is supposed to protect us and ensure our liberty and equality, but often fails because our inequality and lack of freedom come from differences in *social power*, not from differences in our formal legal standing before the law.

It seems to me that educational institutions are being viewed, and rapidly becoming, more and more like the state: Students and faculty are becoming increasingly subordinated to the will of administrators. There seems to be no other recourse for creating change on campus but to appeal to those administrators, who we pray will respond to us. The difficulty, of course, is that it is the professional obligation of those administrators to place the needs of the individuals on campus as subordinate to the needs of the institution—a dynamic we see very clearly played out in *The Hunting Ground*.

I am skeptical, then, about relying on educational institutions to solve the problem of sexual assault on campus precisely because it gives those institutions too much power in deciding how sexual assault should be handled. This is not to say, of course, that educational institutions have no responsibility to provide safe and equal access to education to all their students—they do. However, it is to caution against seeing college administrators as being able to solve the problem of sexual assault on campus. It's also a call not to shift our own ethical responsibility and political power to others.

Luckily, we can see in *The Hunting Ground* an alternative model of ethics and grassroots democratic activism that is not entirely reliant on institutional response—whether of the state or colleges and universities. The really prescient moments in the film are not the scenes about college presidents or law enforcement agencies, but rather Pino and Clark's strategy of "putting a face and a name" to the reality of sexual assault. Beyond simply "humanizing" victims of sexual assault, to witness these people tell their stories is to be asked to face them and respond to their vulnerability and their suffering. In these moments, we turn our attention away from fraternity chapters and football coaches, and are called to be responsive in a way that simply cannot be written into law or educational codes of conduct. This is the place where I found the largest possibility for a transformative shift in how we respond to sexual assault both on and off campus. By shifting the focus away from the responsibility of powerful others, we can reclaim our own responsibility, our ability to respond—to survivors of sexual assault. This is, in my view, to claim a kind of power that is therefore not reliant on institutions to make change at all.

All one has to do is watch Pino and Clark to see this power work, and also to see the ethical valence at the core of it. This is the "moral higher ground in higher education that is just sitting vacant" that psychologist David Lisak speaks of in the film. Yet, where he calls for college presidents to inhabit that higher ground, I am arguing that this moral high ground is available to all of us in contemporary American society. It is imperative that we all take responsibility for sexual violence, on and off college campuses. Pino and Clark can serve as our ethical models here; their real power comes not from making the state or these educational institutions be accountable, but from their own responsiveness to survivors of sexual assault, one that acknowledges survivors as their ethical responsibility, too.

Lisa C. Knisely, PhD, is freelance writer and editor. Her primary academic research focus is on gender, violence, and ethics, but she also writes about sexuality and body politics, as well as social identity and food. She is currently an assistant professor of the liberal arts at the Pacific Northwest College of Art in Portland.

6

A Conversation with the Filmmakers

In their two most recent films, *The Hunting Ground* and *The Invisible War*, Kirby Dick and Amy Ziering stand back and let their subjects do the talking—and this is one of the things that makes their work so effective. In *The Invisible War*, the subjects are women and men in the military, in *The Hunting Ground* they're students, and in both films their frank retelling of their assaults— and the way they were treated by the institutions charged with protecting them—are scorching and unforgettable. These stories are combined with statistics about sexual assault and interviews of experts to put the issue in context, and the overall impact makes the films impossible to forget.

Dick and Ziering are less willing to talk about themselves—out of modesty, in part, but also because they're constantly in motion: putting the finishing touches on the film, calling sources, traveling to yet another screening, meeting with backers, planning their next project. I sat down with them in their busy office on a quiet street in Los Angeles, where, between conference calls and editing sessions, they talked to me about gender roles on college campuses, rape denial, and the making of *The Hunting Ground*.

—*Constance Matthiessen*

Connie: What is it about the campus environment that enables and encourages sexual violence?

Amy: There are several factors that create perfect-storm conditions for the proliferation of these crimes. For one thing, college campuses are target-rich environments, meaning there is a transient population of young people living together in close quarters, many of whom start college with little sexual experience or social savvy. Additionally there is often a heavy party culture at these schools, providing ample opportunity for the commission of these crimes.

On top of all this, many college administrators are prone to believing the same myths as the wider population: they mistakenly think sexual assaults happen in a "gray area," that they are just about a "miscommunication" or a "bad hookup." As a result, these administrators often tend to blame the victim rather than respond appropriately. This combination of factors can make schools hunting grounds for savvy predators who know how to exploit these elements to their advantage. We know that a disproportionate number of sexual assaults are committed by repeat offenders, and that once they are embedded in these target rich environments, if nothing is done to stop them, they will commit these crimes over and over again.

Connie: Can you talk about the change in public awareness of campus sexual assault when you started the film compared to today?

Kirby: When we started exploring the idea of the film in the fall of 2012, the issue of campus sexual assault was just beginning to be covered. The general public was not aware of it as a national issue.

People were focused on individual campuses and individual cases, and that's how it was being reported. It wasn't considered a systemic problem and it wasn't being treated that way. That was also true when we made *The Invisible War;* assault in the military wasn't initially seen as part of a larger systemic problem.

So the climate has really changed since we started making *The Hunting Ground*: People are now beginning to see it as a national issue. It's a problem that is happening everywhere: at Ivy League schools, athletic schools, small private schools, religious schools. No campus is exempt.

Connie: In the film, you talked about the fifties attitudes on college campuses. Can you explain what you mean by that?
Amy: I assumed college would be a more enlightened environment today than it was when I was in school in the eighties, and in many ways it is. But I also found campuses to be surprisingly sexist. The social mores are often gender-bifurcated in a way that seems anachronistic. I suspect it has to do with the rise of a celebrity culture in which women's bodies and appearance are valorized, highly misogynistic and gender-violent music videos, and mainstream media narratives with reductive and objectifying roles for women. At schools we often found there were dress codes for women at parties (but not the men), and bouncers who would allow women entry based solely on their appearance. It wasn't uncommon for fraternity parties to have theme names like "CEOs and 'Ho's," or "Playboy Mansion." We were surprised to find that these regressive and sexist attitudes were prevalent at all the schools we visited, from the most progressive to the most conservative.

I was also surprised to find that these regressive and sexist attitudes were prevalent at all the schools we visited, from the most progressive to the most conservative. And I was surprised by how muted the analysis of this sexist culture was. Even students who were critical would say things like, "This sucks but there's nothing I can do to change it. This is just the way it is."

Kirby: Many people don't realize that there has been a dramatic increase in the popularity of fraternities in recent years. Fraternities experienced a drop in popularity in the Sixties and Seventies, and their membership went down. But in the early Eighties they began gaining ground again, and their membership has increased nearly 50 percent over the last decade. Today fraternity parties dominate the social scene at many institutions—including very progressive ones. Fraternities have the hottest parties on many campuses, and that's where many sexual assaults occur.

Amy: I think that fraternities are more popular now because we have so few support structures left in our society. There is a lot of social and economic insecurity, and that's led to a rise in the number of students joining fraternities, because they provide them with a built-in community. And fraternity culture has also contributed to this shift towards more objectifying views of women.

Connie: Is sexual assault on campus a new problem or is it something that has been going on for a long time?
Kirby: In terms of campus sexual assault, the numbers have been consistent over time: More than one in five women experience sexual assault while they are in college. It's always been a problem.

Connie: What surprised you most when you started interviewing students who had been assaulted?
Kirby: We were astonished by how many survivors we came across. Although all of them were happy a film was being made on the

subject, many were reluctant to be interviewed at first because they had faced such a negative response from their school when they first came forward.

We were also surprised that it didn't matter what kind of school it was; all of the administrators were doing a poor job when it came to dealing with these assaults. Berkeley and Occidental were as bad as the major football schools. We found that the colleges were doing everything they could to protect the image of their institution—and not taking care of the students who had been attacked. We didn't interview a single survivor whose college did the right thing from start to finish in terms of supporting the student and investigating the incident. Instead, administrators usually did everything they could to cover up these crimes, even if it meant that assailants could continue to remain on campus and the survivors' educations were jeopardized.

We saw it over and over: When a student came forward to report an assault, administrators would go into damage-control mode. They would treat the assault as if it were an isolated case. They would suggest the survivor had something do to with it, or warn the student not to talk to anyone about it. Often they would promise that they would take care of it, yet the case would drag on for months. And most of these college officials are still in their jobs today.

To be clear, no administrator wants this to happen on their campus, and we did come across some administrators who wanted their schools to address the problem. These were not administrators at the upper echelons of the universities; these were the people who see these problems on the ground every day. They knew these cases were not being investigated properly but they couldn't do anything about it. The best they could do was offer the student support. But those administrators were the exception, not the rule.

Connie: Was it hard to get college leaders to talk to you?

Amy: It was harder to get college presidents to talk to us for this film than it was to get Pentagon officials to talk to us for *The Invisible War*. We reached out to more than 30 college presidents, and nearly all of them either didn't respond or refused to talk to us.

Connie: What about college faculty?

Amy: We had started the film thinking we'd see faculty members on the front lines of this issue, but for the most part they weren't. We found that faculty were reluctant to speak out publicly on this issue, and that those who did, as we show in our film, were often branded as troublemakers and punished. Untenured faculty members, who have no job security, were particularly vulnerable.

Connie: If a few college presidents took a strong stand and came down hard on perpetrators, do you think that would make a difference?

Amy: It would make a huge difference. When we were doing research for *The Invisible War* which looked at sexual assault in the military, subjects we interviewed would say, "I had a good experience at this base, but a bad experience at that one," and when we asked what was different between the two bases, they would always point to the commander. The climate set by the commander greatly impacted the rates of violence and harassment on the bases. If everyone knew the commander didn't tolerate sexual harassment and punished assault crimes, then they were much less likely to happen in that unit.

In the same way, if students and perpetrators knew that college administrators took this problem seriously and wouldn't turn a blind eye when it happened, it would have a tremendous impact.

It would shift the campuses' climate and the culture would be less likely to give cover to these crimes. It would also send the message to survivors that it's safe to talk about what happened to them. When campus administrators encourage transparency and conversation regarding sexual assault, survivors are able to heal faster and the whole community becomes safer and healthier.

Connie: These situations must be particularly hard for parents.
Kirby: Parents want to believe their school will act in the best interest of the children. And for parents, their child's safety at college is obviously the most important thing. When their child is assaulted, when this awful thing happens, parents naturally assume the school will jump in to help their child and go after the perpetrator. The parents we interviewed were shocked to find that the schools either at best ignored them, or at worst were hostile and uncooperative. The parents we talked to were devastated by the entire experience.
Amy: These crimes don't happen in isolation; they have a domino effect. They hurt not just the survivors but parents, siblings, and friends. It's a train wreck for everyone involved.

Connie: There has been a major backlash against sexual assault survivors in the media and elsewhere. Why do you think denial of this issue is so widespread?
Amy: It's very strange that there is so much hostility toward people who just want to report a crime. As you know, the rates of false reporting of sexual assault crimes are the same as they are for most other crimes in our society. Yet you don't see people doubting or blaming people who come forward to report thefts or battery, but that's what happens routinely to people who report sexual assault.

Kirby: We've been astonished at the amount of push-back there has been on this issue. There are bloggers and others in the media who jump in whenever there is an opportunity to deny that this is a systemic problem. I think it's an indication of how deep-seated the denial of sexual assault remains. It may be a primal reaction to deny that this occurs because it is so threatening. I think it comes from a primitive, false idea that women who have been raped are damaged goods. You see it in some areas of the Middle East, where women who are raped are shunned, or even killed. I think that, as a society, we are always going to have to fight rape denial. It's like racism: We're always going to have to struggle against it if we want to eradicate it.

Connie: Have you been surprised by some of the blowback the film has received?
Kirby: Well, we did make the deliberate choice to name names and call out dozens of powerful institutions for their malfeasance, something reformers had been reluctant to do because of the power of these institutions. So it's not surprising there has been some pushback. What surprised us is how disingenuous it's been and how so many people, from trolls to opinion writers to professors, have tried to discredit the film and deny that sexual assault in college is a real problem in spite of the evidence.

When we made *The Invisible War*, the military viewed it as a critique, not an attack, and there wasn't this concerted effort to deny how serious the problem is. When we made a film about sexual abuse in the Catholic Church, again, no one said it wasn't a real problem. But when *The Hunting Ground* was released, suddenly opinion writers, attorneys, and law professors were claiming that the statistics could not be trusted. Why such a different response? I think a major reason is that it's an issue of class. It's acceptable to speak about soldiers or priests committing rape, but when one begins charging that many entitled middle-class and upper-class white men attending elite institutions are rapists, society circles the wagons and insists that it cannot be true, that these women are lying.

As I was making this film, I kept asking myself, *Why has this problem persisted for so long*? I think part of the answer is that our liberal institutions—the press, the legal profession, and higher education, for example—perpetuate the problem by denying its existence and resisting reform in much the way conservative institutions do. If, decades earlier, the Ivy League schools had made real efforts to address this issue on their campuses, their success would have pressured the rest of our colleges and universities to change. And if the press and the legal profession had been more proactive, that would have helped accelerate that change. But these institutions have failed the country on this issue. (To its credit, over the last couple of years the press has become much better in how it covers college sexual assault.)

In the sixties, liberal institutions played a critical role in reducing discrimination in this country. Attorneys, journalists, college faculty, and students participated in the Freedom Rides, joining with black and white activists in the South to confront the problem. This kind of response to college sexual assault should have happened decades ago, and it can still happen now: a forceful and sustained demand from these institutions for justice and for the protection of the civil rights of our students. (The right to attend college without the risk of sexual assault is a civil right.) Where are the Freedom Riders on this issue? We profiled some in our film—the visionary and courageous student activists out there—and it's now time they are joined and supported by the rest of society.

Connie: Did the *Rolling Stone* article have a major impact? Do you think it has given rape deniers ammunition?

Amy: It has had a seismic impact. But to me it's symptomatic of our culture's misinformed attitudes about sexual assault. The UVA article has been used to discredit the whole issue, and to imply that survivors on the whole aren't telling the truth. It's important to note that we've had many other examples of poor journalism over the years, but they then aren't used to discredit an entire issue. [Former NBC anchor] Brian Williams's report on the Chinook helicopter, for example, called into question his journalism; it didn't call into question whether there was a war going on.

The *Rolling Stone* article was very poorly reported, but let's not forget that the University of Virginia is still under a Title IX investigation, and there have been many reports of rape on its campus. There is clearly a sexual assault problem at UVA, and it surprises me that people aren't more concerned about the dozens and perhaps hundreds of assaults that are happening every year on that campus than one flawed magazine report.

Connie: Because of growing awareness of this issue, colleges are introducing sexual assault education programs. Do you think that will make a difference?

Amy: Studies show that education programs do make a difference. But in addition to these programs, colleges need to have better procedures in place to investigate and adjudicate these crimes so that the criminals on these campuses can't commit them in the first place.

Connie: Are you hopeful that this could be a watershed moment: that college administrators are taking action on the

issue, and that rates of assaults on campus will be lower five to 10 years from now?

Amy: Yes, I am hopeful, that we may be in a transformative moment in our culture. The way the issue is being talked about in the mainstream media is slowly beginning to shift and survivors seem to be gaining more support and empathy in the press.

Kirby: I think both *The Invisible War* and *The Hunting Ground* have helped raise awareness of the issue. There is something about hearing the experiences of survivors and seeing their faces on camera that is very powerful. In the same way that it's hard for people to hold on to homophobic attitudes once they get to know people who are gay, it's much harder to reflexively doubt people once you hear their stories. That's why the survivors who had the courage to speak up in both *The Invisible War* and *The Hunting Ground* are so important. The cumulative impact of those stories is what's changing our understanding of sexual assault from an individual to a systemic problem.

Obama and Biden have been excellent on this issue. I give them a lot of credit for speaking out forcefully and repeatedly on this issue, and pressuring colleges and universities to initiate major policy changes. And the Justice Department has launched Title IX investigations at campuses around the country. I think what this administration has done around sexual assault is historic, and I don't think they get enough credit for how important their campaign has been to help create change. Hopefully the next administration will keep the momentum going.

Connie: Can you talk about your partnership as filmmakers? How did you start working together?

Amy: I was working on a film on the French philosopher Jacques Derrida (*Derrida*, 2002) and a friend invited me to see a rough cut of Kirby's second film. I thought it was really smart and sophisticated in ways that resonated with the work of Derrida. So we decided to collaborate, and we've worked together on and off for the last two decades. Now we have a partnership and a company: Chain Camera Pictures.

In terms of how we work, it depends on the subject of the film, but it's always highly collaborative and nonhierarchical. For example, while I did most of the interviews for this film and for *The Invisible War*, Kirby came in at the end and asked a lot of follow up questions. So we tag team—it's great to have two sets of ears listening to and engaging with film subjects—I think our films are stronger thanks to the collaborative way we work.

Connie: Which film was harder to make in terms of the difficulty of the material—*The Hunting Ground* or *The Invisible War*?

Amy: They were equally hard. This kind of psychic pain is extremely hard to process. The stories are harrowing and stay with you long after the filming ends. In *The Hunting Ground* the subjects were younger, and as a parent I could identify with them and with their parents as I have children in college. The military film was not a culture I am part of, but the women and men's stories broke my heart. The stories of everyone in both these films still haunt me.

Connie: Can you talk about the reaction to *The Hunting Ground* when you've held screenings around the country?

Amy: The reaction has been nothing short of remarkable. We've shown our movies on campuses for the last twenty years and we've never seen responses like this. We've had packed audiences, standing ovations, and requests to keep the DVD so they can schedule additional screenings. And tremendous gratitude on the part of survivors, students, family members, loved ones, and administrators who are grateful to finally have a tool with which they can explain what they are seeing daily, and can use to motivate their schools to change.

Connie: Is there one thing you would like people to take away from *The Hunting Ground*?

Kirby: I'd like people to walk away with the understanding that campus sexual assault isn't an individual matter but a systemic problem.

Amy: I'd also like people to start treating the crime of sexual assault the way they treat any other crime. If someone experiences a carjacking or gets robbed, we don't question their story, or imply that they somehow brought it on themselves. Sexual assault survivors need to be responded to in the same way—with empathy, support, and legitimate efforts to bring their perpetrator to justice. Failure to respond in this way causes immeasurable harm to survivors, their families, and our society as a whole.

7

The Numbers Don't Lie:
The Statistics of Sexual Assault in College

by Kirby Dick

There's been a great deal of debate around sexual assault on college campuses, particularly the figure that one in five or more women are sexually assaulted while in college. Self-proclaimed experts, opinion writers, and even some professors have tried to cast doubt on these studies, claiming the science is flawed.

The truth is that nearly all of this debate has been unnecessary and distracting, since the one in five statistic has been repeatedly established in dozens of national and single school studies. In fact, since 1987, six national studies—including one released in early 2016 by the Department of Justice—show that as many as one in four college women are sexually assaulted in college:

Koss, Gidycz, Wisniewski (1987)
3,187 women in 32 institutions

More than 25% of undergraduate women sexually victimized

Fisher, Cullen, Turner (2000)
4,446 women in two- and four-year institutions
16% of women sexually victimized during the current academic year

Ford, Soto-Marquez (2015)
2,345 women in 21 institutions
25% of women sexually assaulted

Washington Post-Kaiser Family Foundation (2015)
514 women in several hundred institutions
20% of undergraduate women sexually assaulted

Association of American Universities (AAU) (2015)
89,115 women in 27 institutions
23% of undergraduate women sexually assaulted

National Institute of Justice (NIJ) (2016)
15,000 women in 9 institutions
25% of undergraduate women sexually assaulted

Another criticism that commentators like to put forward is that the category for sexual assault is too broad, and includes everything from forced kissing to rape. It's important to remember that each one of these assaults is a crime, and many are felonies. More importantly, there is an astonishingly high percentage, between 11 percent and 16 percent, of women in college who are victims of rape and attempted rape.
Koss, Gidycz, Wisniewski (1987)—Rape 16%

Fisher, Cullen, Turner (2000)—Rape or attempted rape 12%

Kilpatrick, Resnick, Ruggiero, Conoscenti, McCauley (2007)—
    Rape or attempted rape 12%

Association of American Universities (2015)—Rape 11%

National Institute of Justice (2016)—Rape 4% (in one academic
    year only)

This shows a woman has between a one-in-nine and one-in-six chance that she will experience rape or attempted rape in college.

Some critics claim the lower response rate of some of the studies invalidates their findings. They argue, without evidence, that people who've been assaulted will be more likely to respond to a sexual assault survey than people who haven't been assaulted. But an equally strong argument can be made that people who are assaulted would be less likely to take the survey because answering dozens of questions about their sexual assault would be emotionally retraumatizing for them.

In fact, the four national studies with very high response rates (Koss—98.5%, Fisher—86.5%, Ford 100%, and NIJ—54%) show the highest rates of assault. Jennifer Freyd, a highly regarded researcher at the University of Oregon, confirmed this correlation again when she analyzed a 26-school AAU study and demonstrated that schools with higher response rates had slightly higher rates of sexual assault.

There is one outlier study that critics invariably point to: the National Crime Victimization Survey (NCVS), which found a much lower rate of sexual assault. What they don't disclose is that this study has been severely criticized by the National Academies of Sciences, which—in a 278-page report—unequivocally concludes that the NCVS sexual assault numbers are unreliable.

The National Academies of Sciences report lists more than a dozen ways in which the NCVS study fails to employ best practices, including:

- Not counting sexual assault while incapacitated, which in some surveys accounts for more than 50 percent of sexual assault on college campuses.
- Erroneously basing its calculations on an average student attending college for 3.5 years, when in fact the average student now takes nearly six years to graduate, resulting in a potential undercount up to 40 percent.
- Contacting students primarily using land lines and not cell phones, which are much more commonly used by college students.
- Conducting interviews in the home, often within earshot of family members, which discourages students responding to questions about sexual assault.

Why has every opinion writer who has based their argument on the NCVS study failed to mention the critique by the National Academy of Sciences? Either they are unaware of the report, in which case they haven't done the most basic due diligence, or they are aware of it and have deliberately chosen not to inform their readership because the critique would undermine their argument. Either way, the omission discredits their conclusions.

This cynical attempt to manipulate public opinion and convince this country that the problem is overblown is very reminiscent of the debate around global warming. For decades, scientists have shown that human activity is contributing to a rapid rise in the earth's temperature, yet climate change–denying pundits continue to claim this is untrue and that we have nothing to be concerned about. In fact, one of the most prominent of these rape-denying pundits, Emily Yoffe, is also a climate change denier. In an article about the Academy Award–winning documentary *The Inconvenient Truth*, which discusses global warming, Yoffe writes that it is "hard to believe assertions that the science on the future of our climate is set-tled when climate scientists can't agree about the present" and "just because something can be plotted on an X and Y axis does not make it the whole truth."

But the truth is that we can, and must, rely on scientists to analyze human behavior on college campuses, and denying their expertise is a sure path to tragedy. Those who attempt to discredit the work of these scientists do much more than mislead the public. By encouraging our country to ignore this crisis, they contribute to the continuation of the problem. It's time we come together to move beyond these harmful misinformation campaigns, acknowledge this crisis, and create real and effective change for the sake of our nation's college students.

8

How to Get Involved

American Association of University Women—http://www.aauw.org/
Offers an "Ending Campus Sexual Assault Toolkit" and other
resources.

Breakthrough—http://us.breakthrough.tv/
Strives to prevent violence against women by transforming the
norms and cultures worldwide.

Culture of Respect—https://cultureofrespect.naspa.org/
Videos, apps, tools for activists, and other information on campus
sexual assault.

End Rape on Campus (EROC)—http://endrapeoncampus.org/
Support for assault survivors and information on Title IX and other
tools.

Faculty Against Rape (FAR)—http://www.facultyagainstrape.net/
Resources and support for faculty who oppose campus sexual
assault.

Futures Without Violence—http://www.futureswithoutviolence.
org/
Provides groundbreaking programs, policies, and campaigns to
end violence against women and children around the world.

It's On Us—http://itsonus.org/
Launched by President Obama and Vice President Biden with the
White House to end sexual assault on college campuses.

Know Your IX—http://knowyourix.org/
Information on Title IX, the Clery Act, and other ways to address
campus sexual assault.

MaleSurvivor—http://www.malesurvivor.org/
Information and support for adult male victims of sexual assault.

Man Up—https://manupcampaign.org/
A global campaign to activate youth to stop violence against
women and girls.

Men Can Stop Rape—http://www.mencanstoprape.org/
Men working to stop violence against women.

National Sexual Violence Resource Center—http://www.nsvrc.
org/
Strives to provide leadership in preventing and responding to
sexual violence.

Not Alone—https://www.notalone.gov/

A government website launched at the same time as the White House
Task Force to Protect Students from Sexual Assault.

NO MORE—http://nomore.org/
A campaign to raise public awareness and engage bystanders around
ending domestic violence and sexual assault.

One in Four—http://www.oneinfourusa.org/
Education programs to prevent campus sexual assault.

Rape, Abuse, & Incest National Network (RAINN)—https://www.
rainn.org/
Offers a national hotline for assault survivors, access to local crisis
centers, and other information on sexual violence.

Students Active for Ending Rape (SAFER)—http://www.safercampus.
org/home
Supports student-led anti-assault campaigns with an online
library, a campus sexual assault database, and campus
teach-ins.

The Clery Center for Security on Campus—http://clerycenter.org/
Provides trainings and other information to promote campus safety.

Ultraviolet | http://www.weareultraviolet.org/
A growing community of people who work to expand women's
rights.

Find more information and resources at *The Hunting Ground*
website—http://www.thehuntinggroundfilm.com/resources

Film Information

KIRBY DICK—Selected Filmography

2015 *THE HUNTING GROUND*
A monumental examination of the cover-up of sexual assaults on
U.S. campuses and the rise of a new student movement

Title: Director, Writer
Distributor: Radius Films, The Weinstein Company, CNN Films
Premiere: 2015 Sundance Film Festival

AWARDS
Shortlist—Best Documentary—Academy Awards 2016
Nominee—Best Original Song—Academy Awards 2016
Winner—Stanley Kramer Award—Producers Guild of America
Awards 2016

2012 *THE INVISIBLE WAR*
A groundbreaking investigation into the epidemic of rape in the
U.S. military

Title: Director, Writer
Distributor: Cinedigm
Premiere: 2012 Sundance Film Festival

AWARDS

Nominee—Best Feature Documentary—Academy Awards 2013

Winner—Best Documentary—Emmy Awards 2014

Winner—Outstanding Investigative Journalism-Long Form—
Emmy Awards 2014

Winner—Best Feature Documentary—Independent Spirit Awards
2013

Winner—Best U.S. Documentary, Audience Award—Sundance
Film Festival 2012

Winner—George Foster Peabody Award 2013

2009 *OUTRAGE*

A powerful exposé of the hypocrisy of powerful closeted politicians
who legislate against gay rights

Title: Director, Writer

Distributor: Magnolia Films

Premiere: 2009 Tribeca Film Festival

AWARDS

Nominee—Outstanding Investigative Journalism—Emmy Awards
2010

2006 *THIS FILM IS NOT YET RATED*

A breakthrough investigation into the powerful Motion Picture
Association of America and its secretive and corrupt film
rating system

Title: Director, Writer

Distributor: IFC Films

Premiere: 2006 Sundance Film Festival

AWARDS
Nominee—Best Documentary—Broadcast Critic Awards 2007

2005 *TWIST OF FAITH*
The powerful story of a fireman, abused as a child by a Catholic
priest, who breaks his silence and confronts his church

Title: Director
Distributor: HBO Films
Premiere: 2005 Sundance Film Festival

AWARDS
Nominee—Best Feature Documentary—Academy Awards 2005
Winner—Audience Award—Amnesty International Film Festival
2005

2002 *DERRIDA*
A complex portrait of the world-renowned French philosopher
Jacques Derrida, known as the founder of Deconstruction

Title: Director
Distributor: Zeitgeist Films
Premiere: 2002 Sundance Film Festival

AWARDS
Winner—Golden Gate Award—San Francisco Film Festival 2002

2001 *CHAIN CAMERA*
A riveting portrayal of contemporary teenage life as seen through
the eyes and cameras of students at a large urban high school
in Los Angeles

Title: Director
Distributor: HBO Documentary Films
Premiere: 2001 Sundance Film Festival

1997 *SICK: THE LIFE & DEATH OF BOB FLANAGAN, SUPERMASOCHIST*

A deeply moving portrait of one of the most unique artists of the 20th century and his explorations of the limits of pain, sexuality, love, and death

Title: Director
Distributor: Lions Gate Films
Premiere: 1997 Sundance Film Festival

AWARDS
Winner—Special Jury Prize—Sundance Film Festival 1997
Winner—Grand Prize—Los Angeles Film Festival 1997
Winner—Best Documentary Nomination—IFP Spirit Awards 1997

1996 *GUY* (dramatic)

The story of a woman documentary filmmaker who randomly selects a strange man and relentlessly follows him with her camera into the most intimate parts of his life

Title: Writer
Directed by Michael Lindsay-Hogg
Starring Vincent D'Onofrio and Hope Davis
Distributor: Polygram Filmed Entertainment
Premiere: 1996 Venice International Film Festival

1986 *PRIVATE PRACTICES: THE STORY OF A SEX SURROGATE*

An intimate profile of two men and the sex surrogate who helps them, as they go through a course of sex surrogate therapy that becomes progressively more intimate

Title: Director
Distributor: Kino International
Premiere: 1986 Filmex Los Angeles

AWARDS
Winner—Best Documentary Award—USA Film Festival 1985
Winner—Best Documentary Award—Atlanta Film Festival 1985

PERSONAL AWARDS
2012 Nestor Almendros Prize for Courage in Filmmaking
2013 Ridenhour Documentary Film Prize
2013 USC Price Guardian Award for Vision and Leadership
2015 Distinguished Service & Excellence in Film Award Institute on Violence, Abuse, and Trauma

EDUCATION
California Institute of the Arts, Valencia, CA
American Film Institute, Los Angeles, CA

AMY ZIERING—Filmography

2015 *THE HUNTING GROUND*

A monumental examination of the cover up of sexual assaults on U.S. campuses and the rise of a new student movement

Title: Producer (also received a "Film By" credit along with
     Director Kirby Dick)
Distributor: Radius Films, The Weinstein Company, CNN Films
Premiere: 2015 Sundance Film Festival

AWARDS
Shortlist—Best Documentary—Academy Awards 2016
Nominee—Best Original Song—Academy Awards 2016
Winner—Stanley Kramer Award—Producers Guild of America
     Awards 2016

2012 *THE INVISIBLE WAR*

A groundbreaking investigation into the epidemic of rape in the
     U.S. military

Title: Producer (also received a "Film By" credit along with
     Director Kirby Dick)
Distributor: Cinedigm
Premiere: 2012 Sundance Film Festival

AWARDS
Nominee—Best Feature Documentary—Academy Awards 2013
Winner—Best Documentary—Emmy Awards 2014
Winner—Outstanding Investigative Journalism-Long Form—
     Emmy Awards 2014
Winner—Best Feature Documentary—Independent Spirit Awards
     2013
Winner—Best U.S. Documentary, Audience Award—Sundance
     Film Festival 2012

Winner—George Foster Peabody Award 2013

2009 *OUTRAGE*

A powerful exposé of the hypocrisy of powerful closeted
 politicians who legislate against gay rights

Title: Producer
Distributor: Magnolia Films
Premiere: 2009 Tribeca Film Festival

AWARDS
Nominee—Outstanding Investigative Journalism—Emmy Awards
 2010

2006 *THE MEMORY THIEF* (Dramatic)

A melancholy journey into madness as a young man's obsession
 with the Holocaust leads to him to take on the memories of
 survivors as if they were his own

Title: Producer
Distributor: 7th Art Releasing

AWARDS
Winner—Digital Feature Award—Edmonton International Film
 Festival 2006
Winner—Grand Jury Prize—Red Rock Film Festival 2006

2002 *DERRIDA*

A complex portrait of the world-renowned French philosopher
 Jacques Derrida, known as the founder of Deconstruction

Title: Producer
Distributor: Zeitgeist Films
Premiere: 2002 Sundance Film Festival

AWARDS
Winner—Golden Gate Award—San Francisco Film Festival 2002

1998 *TAYLOR'S CAMPAIGN*
The story of Ron Taylor, a homeless person who ran for a seat on
 the Santa Monica City Council

Title: Producer
Distributor: Self-distributed by director Richard Cohen

AWARDS
Winner—Special Jury Award—Big Muddy Film Festival 1998
Winner—Reel Award—Arizona International Film Festival 1998

PERSONAL AWARDS
2012 Nestor Almendros Prize for Courage in Filmmaking
2013 Ridenhour Documentary Film Prize
2013 Gracie Award for Outstanding Producer—News/Non-Fiction

EDUCATION
Ziering graduated Phi Beta Kappa and Summa Cum Laude from
 Amherst College in 1984 and then was in a PhD program
 at Yale in Comparative Literature, where she studied with
 Jacques Derrida, Barbara Johnson, Shoshana Felman, and
 Geoffrey Hartman.
B.A. Amherst College, Amherst, MA
M.A., M. Phil. Yale University, New Haven, CT

The Hunting Ground Production Credits

Written & Directed by | Kirby Dick
Produced by | Amy Ziering
Executive Producers | Tom Quinn

Jason Janego

Vinnie Malhotra

Amy Entelis

Regina K. Scully

Amy and Paul Blavin

Ruth Ann Harnisch

Robert A. Compton

Mark and Barbara Gerson

Sukey Novogratz

Maria Cuomo Cole

Anne O'Shea and Brian
  Quattrini

Julie and Sébastien
  Lépinard

Sarah Johnson

Barbara Dobkin

Ted Dintersmith and
  Elizabeth Hazard

Jacki Zehner

Nicole Boxer

Jennifer Siebel Newsom

Wendy Schmidt

Julie Smolyansky

	Geralyn White Dreyfous
	Dan Cogan
Co-Producers	Bonnie Greenberg
	Nicole Ehrlich
Investigative Producer	Amy Herdy
Editors	Doug Blush, A.C.E.
	Derek Boonstra
	Kim Roberts, A.C.E.
Original Score by	Miriam Cutler
"Til it Happens to You"	Written by Diane Warren and Lady Gaga
	Performed by Lady Gaga
Music Supervisors	Bonnie Greenberg
	Christy Gerhart
Sound Design	Richard King
Design & Animation	Bil White
Cinematography	Thaddeus Wadleigh
	Aaron Kopp
Interviewers	Amy Ziering
	Kirby Dick
	Amy Herdy
Additional Writing	Amy Ziering
Supervising Producer	Courtney Sexton
Associate Producers	Ian Rose
	Audrey Logan
	Chao Thao
	Doug Blush
Associate Editor	Edward Patrick Alva
Assistant Editor	Sally Volkmann
Production Coordinators	Chao Thao

Ian Rose

Melissa Echeverry

Associate Investigative Producer Linda Himelstein

Sources

Introduction

Flanagan, Caitlin, "The Dark Power of Fraternities," *The Atlantic*, http://www.theatlantic.com/magazine/archive/2014/03/the-dark-power-of-fraternities/357580/, 03.2014.

Kingkade, Tyler, "Fewer Than One-Third of Campus Sexual Assault Cases Result in Expulsion," *The Huffington Post,* 09.29.2014.

U.S. Senate Subcommittee on Financial & Contracting Oversight, "Sexual Violence on Campus: How Too Many Institutions of Higher Education Are Failing to Protect Students," http://www.mccaskill.senate.gov/surveyreportwithappendix.pdf, 07.09.2014.

Faculty Against Rape: www.facultyagainstrape.net/.

Dartmouth Change: http://www.dartmouthchange.org/.

Yoffe, Emily, "The College Rape Overcorrection," *Slate,* 12.07.2014.

foxnews.com, "'Accused Is Guilty:' Campus Rape Tribunals Punish Without Proof, Critics Say," http://www.foxnews.com/us/2015/06/20/accused-is-guilty-campus-rape-tribunals-punish-without-proof-say-critics/, 06.20.2015.

Will, George, "Colleges Become Victims of Progressivism," *The Washington Post*, https://www.washingtonpost.com/opinions/george-will-college-become-the-victims-of-progressivism/2014/06/06/e90e73b4-eb50-11e3-9f5c-9075d5508f0a_story.html, 06.06.2014.

Ganim, Sara, "Beyond *Rolling Stone* Story: How Does UVA Handle Campus Sexual Assault?" CNN.com, http://www.cnn.com/2015/04/06/us/uva-sexual-assault-investigation/, 04.06.15.

Harris, Samantha, "One in Five? The White House's Questionable Sexual Assault Data," *Forbes*, http://www.forbes.com/sites/realspin/2014/05/07/one-in-five-the-white-houses-questionable-sexual-assault-data/, 05.07.2014.

Anderson, Nick, and Clement, Scott, "College Sexual Assault: 1 in 5 Women Say They Were Violated," *The Washington Post*, http://www.

washingtonpost.com/sf/local/2015/06/12/1-in-5-women-say-they-were-violated/?wpisrc=al_exclusive, 06.12.2015.

Carey, Kate B., et al. "Incapacitated and Forcible Rape of College Women: Prevalence Across the First Year," CNN, http://i2.cdn.turner.com/cnn/2015/images/05/20/carey_jah_proof.pdf, 05.20.2015.

InsideHigherEd.com, "Survey: 22% of Female Students at Michigan Sexually Assaulted," https://www.insidehighered.com/quicktakes/2015/06/25/survey-22-female-students-michigan-sexually-assaulted, 06.25.2014.

University of Michigan, "Results of 2015 University of Michigan Campus Climate Survey on Sexual Misconduct," https://publicaffairs.vpcomm.umich.edu/wp-content/uploads/sites/19/2015/04/Complete-survey-results.pdf, 04.19.2015.

Voices of Survivors

Interview with Laurie Richer, medical director of San Francisco General Hospital's Trauma Recovery Center, 07.2015.

Interviews conducted for *The Hunting Ground*.

"Sexual Assault in a Football Town" by Amy Herdy

Tallahassee police report.

The Hunting Ground; Bogdanich, Walt, "A Star Player Accused, and a Flawed Rape Investigation," *New York Times*, April 16, 2014, http://www.nytimes.com/interactive/2014/04/16/sports/errors-in-inquiry-on-rape-allegations-against-fsu-jameis-winston.html?_r=0.

Axon, Rachel, "FSU Under Investigation for Handling of Jameis Winston Case," *USA Today*, April 4, 2014, http://www.usatoday.com/story/sports/ncaaf/2014/04/03/jameis-winston-florida-state-rape-investigation-title-ix-civil-rights/7262359/.

Tallahassee police report; Arcia, Gil, "Winston's Accuser Tells a Different Story," *Bucs Blitz*, February 21, 2015, http://tam.scout.com/story/1519974-winston-s-accuser-tells-a-different-story.

Bogdanich, Walt, "A Star Player Accused, and a Flawed Rape Investigation," *New York Times*, April 16, 2014, http://www.nytimes.com/

interactive/2014/04/16/sports/errors-in-inquiry-on-rape-allega-tions-against-fsu-jameis-winston.html?_r=0; *The Hunting Ground*; *Erica Kinsman v. Florida State University Board of Trustees*.

Kinsman v. Florida State University Board of Trustees.

Vaughan, Kevin, "Documents: Police, FSU Hampered Jameis Winston Investigation," Fox News, October 10, 2014, http://www.foxsports.com/college-football/story/jameis-winston-florida-state-tallahas-see-police-hindered-investigation-documents-101014.

"Winston Investigation: Chris Casher Interview," http://www.usatoday.com/videos/sports/ncaaf/acc/2013/12/11/3991823/.

State Attorney's Office report; Schlabach, Mark, "Test Links Winston's DNA to Accuser," ESPN, January 2, 2014, http://espn.go.com/col-lege-football/story/_/id/10009077/dna-analysis-matches-jameis-winston-accuser; *The Hunting Ground*.

Fraternities and Sexual Assault

Flanagan, Caitlin, "The Dark Power of Fraternities," *The Atlantic*, http://www.theatlantic.com/magazine/archive/2014/03/the-dark-power-of-fraternities/357580/, 03.2014.

Contributing Essays
"Sexual Assault and the Media" by Christina Asquith

Reilly, Steve, "Tens of Thousands of Rape Kits Untested Across USA,"*USA Today*, http://www.usatoday.com/story/news/2015/07/16/untested-rape-kits-evidence-across-usa/29902199/, 07.16.2015.

Anderson, Nick, and Clement, Scott, "College Sexual Assault: 1 in 5 Women Say They Were Violated," *The Washington Post*,http://www.washingtonpost.com/sf/local/2015/06/12/1-in-5-women-say-they-were-violated/?wpisrc=al_exclusive, 06.12.2015.

Sherriff, Lucy "'Rape Culture Is a War on Boys on College Campuses', According to Fox News Host Andrea Tantaros," *Huffington Post UK*, http://www.huffingtonpost.co.uk/2015/03/25/rape-culture-is-a-war-on-boys-says-fox-news-host_n_6938248.html, 3.25.2015.

Wilkinson, Jenny, "Sexually Assaulted at UVA," *The New York Times*, http://www.nytimes.com/2015/04/05/opinion/sunday/sexually-assaulted-at-uva.html?_r=0, 04.05.2015.

"Sports on Trial" by Jessica Luther

New, Jake, "No Special Treatment," *Inside Higher Ed*, 08.14.2014.

Peter, Josh, "Former Oklahoma Coach Barry Switzer Admits He Covered Up Minor Charges Against Players," *USA Today*, http://ftw.usatoday.com/2014/10/barry-switzer-misdemeanor-charges, 10.09.14.

McIntire, Mike, and Bogdanich, Walt, "At Florida State, Football Clouds Justice," *The New York Times*, http://www.nytimes.com/2014/10/12/us/florida-state-football-casts-shadow-over-tallahassee-justice.html?_r=0, 10.10.2014.

Autullo, Ryan, Davis, Brian, and Plohetski, Tony, "Strong Indefinitely Suspends Players Charged with Sexual Assault," *Statesman*, http://www.statesman.com/weblogs/bevo-beat/2014/jul/24/two-texas-players-charged-sexual-assault/, 07.24.2014.

"Faculty and the Campus Anti-Rape Movement" by Alissa Ackerman & Caroline Heldman

Krebs, C. P., Lindquist, C.H., Warner, T.D., Fisher, B.S., and Martin, S.L.*The Campus Sexual Assault (CSA) Study*, (2007). This was the report to the federal funding agency, accessed at https://www.ncjrs.gov/pdffiles1/nij/grants/221153.pdf.

Schneck, Ken, "Why Are College Faculty Quiet About Campus Sexual Assault?" *The Huffington Post*, http://www.huffingtonpost.com/ken-schneck-phd/why-are-college-faculty-s_b_6356892.html, 12.24.2014.

Interview with S. Daniel Carter, February 2014

United States Department of Education. "Dear Colleague Letter: Retaliation." Ed.gov. April 24, 2013. Retrieved January 10, 2014 (http://www2.ed.gov/about/offices/list/ocr/letters/colleague-201304.html).

Beusman, Callie, "Colleges Fire and Silence Faculty who Speak Out About Rape," Jezebel.com, June 13, 2014, http://jezebel.com/colleges-silence-and-fire-faculty-who-speak-out-about-r-1586169489. Retrieved June 17, 2014.

Woolington, Josephine, "Scholar's Sexual Violence Study Rejected," *The Register-Guard*, June 11, 2014, retrieved June 11, 2014, http://projects. registerguard.com/rg/news/local/31703535–75/sexual-survey-freyd-violence-university.html.csp.

Anderson, K.J., and Kanner, Melinda "Inventing a Gay Agenda: Students' Perceptions of Lesbian and Gay Professors." *Journal of Applied Social Psychology* 41 (6) (2011): 1538–64.

Gutiérrez y Muhs, G., Flores, Niemann Y., González, C.G., and Harris, A.P. *Presumed Incompetent: The Intersections of Race and Class for Women in Academia*. Logan, Utah: Utah State University Press, 2012.

Bombardieri, Marcella. "Harvard Professor Challenges Denial of Tenure." *The Boston Globe*, June 13, 2014, retrieved June 11, 2014, http://www.bostonglobe.com/metro/2014/06/12/harvard-professor-challenges-tenure-denial/E64ruokHoD1WpokjwsbR3M/story.html.

Rabe Thomas, Jacqueline. "UConn Prof Says Her Support of Outspoken Student May Cost Her Her Job," *The Connecticut Mirror*, November 13, 2013, retrieved June 11, 2014, http://ctmirror.org/uconn-prof-says-her-support-outspoken-student-may-cost-her-her-job/.

Koss, Mary P., and Oros, Cheryl J, "Sexual Experiences Survey: A Research Instrument Investigating Sexual Aggression and Victimization." *Journal of Consulting and Clinical Psychology*, 50(3) (1982): 455–457.

Sanday, P.R. *Fraternity Gang Rape: Sex, Brotherhood, and Privilege on Campus*. New York: New York University Press, 1990.

Kingkade, Tyler, "Education Department Expands Title IX Investigations, Bringing Total to 60 Colleges," *The Huffington Post*, May 28, 2014, retrieved June 3, 2014, http://www.huffingtonpost.com/2014/05/28/education-department-investigations-title-ix_n_5400345.html.

Murphy, Wendy, "Using Title IX's 'Prompt and Equitable' Hearing Requirements to Force Schools to Provide Fair Judicial Proceedings to Redress Sexual Assault on Campus, *New England Law Review*, 40 (2006), http://www.nesl.edu/userfiles/file/lawreview/vol40/4/Murphy.pdf.

"Target Rape on Campus" by Diane Rosenfeld

Original Source: http://harvardlawreview.org/2015/06/uncomfortable-conversations-confronting-the-reality-of-target-rape-on-campus/

1. Alexandra Scheeler, a former member of Princeton's Tiger Inn, wrote about how she had objected to t-shirts that referred to women as "stuck-up c***s." She was dismissed as taking the "joke" too seriously, but maintains that "when jokes repeatedly and consistently mark women as second-class members, they are no longer funny." Alexandra Scheeler, "At Tiger Inn, Women Are the Punch Line," *DAILY PRINCETONIAN*, Dec. 3, 2014, http://dailyprincetonian.com/ opinion /2014/12/at-ti-women-are-the-punch-line [http://perma. cc/4LC4-QXRG].

2. "Incapacitated assault" refers to sexual abuse while "drugged, drunk, passed out, or other- wise incapacitated." NOT ALONE: THE FIRST REPORT OF THE WHITE HOUSE TASK FORCE TO PROTECT STUDENTS FROM SEXUAL ASSAULT 6 (2014) (citing CSA STUDY, *supra* note 1), https://www.notalone.gov/assets/ report.pdf [https://perma.cc/SJT4-75UA] [hereinafter TASK FORCE REPORT]; *see also* DEAN G. KILPATRICK ET AL., NAT'L CRIME VICTIMS RESEARCH & TREATMENT CTR., MED. UNIV. OF S.C., DRUG-FACILITATED, INCAPACITATED, AND FORCIBLE RAPE: A NATIONAL STUDY 2 (2007), https://www.ncjrs.gov/ pdffiles1/nij/grants /219181.pdf [https://perma.cc/PRU5-EK29]. Deliberate administration of drugs in order to facilitate sexual assault is of course not limited to college campuses. For example, more than a dozen women have now reported that they were drugged and then raped by entertainer Bill Cosby. Peter Holley, "Colleges Cut Ties with Bill Cosby as the List of Women Accusing Him of Sexual Assault Hits 20," *Washington Post*, Dec. 1, 2014, http://www.washingtonpost. com/blogs/style-blog/wp/2014/11 /28/colleges-cut-ties-with-bill-cosby-as-the-list-of-women-accusing-him-of-sexual-assault-hits-20 [http://perma.cc/4PV6-RGYG].

3. David Lisak, *Understanding the Predatory Nature of Sexual Violence*, 14 SEXUAL ASSAULT REP. 49, 49–50 (2011). In *The Undetected Rapist*, Lisak describes how men select potential targets based on their vulnerability and innocence, groom them through feigned emotional or social interest, gain their trust, and then incapacitate them through drugs or alcohol and rape them. DAVID LISAK,

THE UNDETECTED RAPIST (2002), http://www.usfk.mil/usfk/
Uploads/SAPR /SAPRMod17_UndetectedRapist.pdf.

4. See, *e.g.*, W.R. Bollen, TOTAL FRAT MOVE (2013) (describ-
    ing fraternity culture, regarding women in sororities as "sorosti-
    tutes," *id.* at 165). A chapter called "Sorostitute Stories" details the
    author's sexual exploitation of women, admitting that he was "a
    rookie in the game of sexual dominance, and the learning had only
    just begun." *Id.* at 169. "Campus was basically a sex commune . . . .
    [T]he odds of getting a girl in bed improved dramatically for even
    the most unsightly scholars. This was even truer for those of us for-
    tunate enough to be members of upstanding Greek organizations
    with tilted moral compasses and a never-ending supply of alcohol."
    Id. at 165.

5. Diane L. Rosenfeld, "Who Are You Calling a 'Ho'?: Challenging the
    Porn Culture on Campus,"in *Big Porn Inc* 41, 42 (Melinda Tankard
    Reist & Abigail Bray eds., 2011) (internal quotation marks omitted).

6. *See, e.g.*, PEGGYREEVESSANDAY, FRATERNITY GANG RAPE
    148(2ded.2007).

7. Some postulate that gang rapes are committed in highly homosocial
    groups of men, perhaps to allay homophobic fears and to dem-
    onstrate a violent, heteronormative sexuality. *See, e.g.*, JEFF BEN-
    EDICT, OUT OF BOUNDS: INSIDE THE NBA'S CULTURE OF
    RAPE, VIOLENCE, AND CRIME (2004); SANDAY, *supra* note 73,
    at 136–37.

8. "Leading Expert on Campus Rape, Sexual Assault Speaks at
    Clark," Clark University, Nov. 19, 2010, http://news.clarku.edu/
    news/2010/11/19/leading-expert-on-campus-rape-sexual-assault-
    speaks-at-clark [http://perma.cc/MY68-MGYA] (reporting on a lec-
    ture by researcher David Lisak, in which he described one fraternity's
    "designated rooms" for isolating victims [internal quotation marks
    omitted]).

9. For a noncomprehensive list of major college football sexual assault
    cases in the last four decades, see Jessica W. Luther, *A List of Col-
    lege Football Rape Cases*, POWER FORWARD (Sept. 26, 2013, 12:06
    PM), http://pwrfwd.net/2013/09/26/a-list-of-college-football-rape-
    cases [http:// perma.cc/B2YY-KBRD].

10. *See* Craig Stevens, *A Review of Literature: Violence by Male Athletes* (2012), http://www.northeastern.edu/sportinsociety/wp-content/uploads/2012/10/ViolenceByMaleAthletes.pdf [http:// perma.cc/58HM-WH7E] (surveying literature).

11. *See* Kimberly M. Trebon, Note, *There Is No "I" in Team: The Commission of Group Sexual Assault by Collegiate and Professional Athletes*, 4 DEPAUL J. SPORTS L. & CONTEMP. PROBS. 65, 72–73 (2007) (citing group loyalty, absence of moral self-scrutiny, sex segregation, and feelings of entitlement as contributing to sexual assault committed by college and professional athletes).

12. For a more extensive discussion of this phenomenon, see Diane L. Rosenfeld, Concluding Remarks, *Changing Social Norms? Title IX and Legal Activism*, 31 HARV. J.L. & GENDER 407 (2008).

13. *See* Walt Bogdanich, "A Star Player Accused, and a Flawed Rape Investigation," *New York Times,* April 16, 2014, http://www.nytimes.com/interactive/2014/04/16/sports/errors-in-inquiry-on-rape -allegations-against-fsu-jameis-winston.html; Marc Tracy, "Jameis Winston Being Sued by Woman Who Accused Him of Rape in 2012," *New York Times,* April 16, 2015, http://www.nytimes.com/2015/04/17/sports/football/jameis-winston-being-sued-by-accuser-in-alleged-rape-in-2012.html.

14. *See* Bogdanich, *supra* note15.

15. *See id.* ("[T]he university did nothing about it, allowing Mr. Winston to play the full season without having to answer any questions.").

16. Cindy Boren, "Laughter at Jameis Winston Press Conference Struck Wrong Note (Video)," *Washington Post*, Dec. 5, 2013, http://www.washingtonpost.com/blogs/early-lead/wp/2013/12/05 /laughter-at-jameis-winston-press-conference-struck-wrong-note-video [http://perma.cc/Q42Q-HYLU]. Winston's case is remarkable for several reasons. The allegations involved three football players who are accused of collaborating in the rape of a young woman who believes she was drugged at a bar and then taken to Winston's apartment, where he raped her first in the bedroom with the door open so that one of his teammates could join in if he wanted to, then in the bathroom. Post-Hearing Memorandum, *supra* note 23, at 5, 15; Bogdanich, *supra* note 61. After the assaults, the woman tweeted

"SOMEONE PLEASE HELP" and was taken to the hospital where she had a rape kit done. Post-Hearing Memorandum, *supra* note 23, at 7. While Winston was under investigation, he and another teammate performed a pro-rape rap song on video. Mike McIntire & Walt Bogdanich, "At Florida State, Football Clouds Justice," *New York Times,* Oct. 10, 2014, http://www.nytimes.com/2014/10/12/us/florida-state-football-casts-shadow-over-tallahassee-justice.html. FSU has shown a pattern of failing to investigate rapes and other irregular activity indicating cover-ups of illegal behavior by football players. *See id.* For an in-depth coverage of this case, see Chapter 2.

17. *See* Jill Martin, "Student Sues University of Oregon, Coach over Alleged Gang-Rape," CNN, Jan. 9, 2015, 9:33 p.m., http://www.cnn.com/2015/01/09/justice/university-of-oregon-title-ix-lawsuit [http://perma.cc/65MM-JVZ7].

18. Jeff Goodman and Andy Katz, "Ducks Ban 3 from Team Activities," ESPN, May 7, 2014, http://espn.go.com/mens-college-basketball/story/_/id/10885689/oregon-ducks-keeping-dominic-artis-bran-don-austin-damyean-dotson-participating-team-activities [http://perma.cc/729N -NNYW]; *see also* Tyler Kingkade, "Oregon Finds 3 Basketball Players Guilty of Sexual Assault, Will Remove Them from Campus," *Huffington Post,* June 23, 2014, 8:59 p.m., http://www.huffingtonpost.com/2014/06/23/oregon-sexual-assault-basketball-players_n_5522915.html [http:// perma.cc/3WYM-UNFY].

19. Kingkade, *supra* note 66. Austin, remarkably, was permitted to transfer to a third institution, where he continued to play basketball. Martin, *supra* note 65.

20. *Simpson v. Univ. of Colo.,* 372 F. Supp. 2d 1229, 1231–32 (D. Colo. 2005) (*reporting plaintiffs' claims that football recruits raped plaintiff and her roommate while the players cheered them on*), *rev'd,* Simpson v. Univ. of Colo. Boulder, 500 F.3d 1170 (10th Cir. 2007).

21. *See* Allison Sherry, "CU Settles Case Stemming from Recruit Scandal," *Denver Post,* Dec. 6, 2007, 1:00 a.m., http://www.denverpost.com/wintersports/ci_7645722 [http://perma.cc/H9ZA-WNGS] (reporting that the University settled with Simpson for $2.5 million and with the second victim for $350,000).

22. *See id.*

23. 529U.S.598(2000).

24. *Id.* At 627.

25. *See id.*

26. *See id.* at 602; *Brzonkala v. Va. Polytechnic Inst. & State Univ.*, 132 F.3d 949, 953–56 (4th Cir. 1997), *vacated*, 169 F.3d 820 (4th Cir. 1999) (en banc).

27. *Morrison*, 529U.S.at 602.

28. *Id.*

29. *Id.*(omission in original)(internal quotationmarks omitted); *Brzonkala*, 132F.3dat953.

30. *Morrison*,529U.S.at602.

31. *Id.*

32. *Brzonkala*, 169 F.3d at 830 (holding that Morrison's actions provided sufficient evidence of gender-based animus "to defeat Morrison's motion to dismiss"); *Brzonkala*, 132 F.3d at 964 ("Virtually all of the earmarks of 'hate crimes' are asserted here . . . ."); *Brzonkala v. Va. Polytechnic & State Univ.*, 935 F. Supp. 779, 785 (W.D. Va. 1996) ("Morrison's actions outwardly evidence gender animus more than many, if not most, situations of rape . . . .").

33. *Morrison*, 529 U.S. at 603.

34. *Brzonkala*, 169 F.3d at 907 (Motz, J., dissenting); David Teel, "Lawsuit Charges Tech Standout," *Daily Press,* March 2, 1996, http://articles. dailypress.com/1996–03-02/sports/9603020075_1_sexual-assault-christy-brzonkala-cornell-brown [http://perma.cc/F5Q5-76V2].

35. Teel, *supra* note 41.

36. *Morrison*, 529 U.S.at 603; *Brzonkala*,132F.3d at 955.

37. "Brzonkala . . . alleges that the procedural irregularities in, as well as the ultimate outcome of, the second hearing were the result of the involvement of Head Football Coach Frank Beamer, as part of a coordinated university plan to allow Morrison to play football in 1995." *Brzonkala*, 132 F.3d at 956.38. *Id.*at955.

39. *Id.*at955.

40. In January 2014, President Obama created the White House Task Force to Protect Students from Sexual Assault to provide leadership and support to make campuses safer and more equal. Press Release, White House Office of the Press Sec'y, Memorandum—Establishing a

White House Task Force to Protect Students from Sexual Assault, Jan. 22, 2014, http://www .whitehouse.gov/the-press-office/2014/01/22/ memorandum-establishing-white-house-task-force -protect-students- sexual-a [https://perma.cc/C7CV-NFE3]. Significant developments from OCR, the enforcement agency responsible for Title IX, include the publication of "Dear Colleague Letters" (DCLs) and subsequent guidance documents to schools. These publications include a DCL on bullying, sexual orientation, and FAQs regarding implementa- tion of the Revised Sexual Harassment Guidance from 2001. *See* sources cited *supra* note 12. The agency has also become transparent in publishing its decisions and revealing the list of schools currently under investigation. *See* Kingkade, *supra* note 25. The Violence Against Women Reauthorization Act of 2013, Pub. L. No. 113–4, 127 Stat. 54 (codified in scattered sections of the U.S. Code), included the Campus Sexual Violence Elimination Act, *id.* § 304, 127 Stat. at 89–92 (codified at 20 U.S.C. § 1092 (2012)), ("Campus SaVE") that sets forth detailed requirements of what schools must report to the government in terms of their compliance with Title IX and the Clery Act, *see* 20 U.S.C. § 1092(f).

41. Diane Rosenfeld, "Schools Must Prevent the Second Rape," *Harvard Crimson*, April 4, 2014.

"Facing Each Other" by Lisa C. Knisely

Beauvoir, Simone de. *The Ethics of Ambiguity*. Secaucus, N.J.: Carol Publishing Group, Citadel Press, 1948.

——— *The Second Sex*. New York: Alfred A. Knopf, 2009.

Brown, Wendy. *States of Injury: Power and Freedom in Late Modernity*. Princeton, N.J.: Princeton University Press, 1995.

Bumiller, Kristin. *In an Abusive State: How Neoliberalism Appropriated the Feminist Movement Against Sexual Violence*. Durham, N.C.: Duke University Press, 2008.

Butler, Judith. *Giving an Account of Oneself*. New York: Fordham University Press, 2005.

——— *Precarious Life: The Powers of Mourning and Violence*. London: Verso, 2004.

Cahill, Ann J. *Rethinking Rape*. Ithaca, N.Y.: Cornell University Press, 2001.

Gavey, Nicola. *Just Sex? The Cultural Scaffolding of Rape*. New York: Routledge, 2005.

Haag, Pamela. "'Putting Your Body on the Line': The Question of Violence, Victims, and the Legacies of Second-Wave Feminism." *Differences: A Journal of Feminist Cultural Studies* 8, no. 2 (1996).

Halley, Janet. *Split Decisions: How and Why to Take a Break from Feminism*. Princeton, N.J.: Princeton University Press, 2006.

Heberle, Renée J. "Rethinking the Social Contract: Masochism and Masculinist Violence." In *Theorizing Sexual Violence*, edited by Renée J. Heberle and Victoria Grace. New York: Routledge, 2009.

Marcus, Sharon. "Fighting Bodies, Fighting Words: A Theory and Politics of Rape Prevention." In *Feminists Theorize the Political*, edited by Joan W. Scott and Judith Butler, 385–403. New York: Routledge, 1992.

Murphy, Ann V. *Violence and Philosophical Imaginary*. Albany, N.Y.: SUNY Press, 2012.

Oliver, Kelly. *Witnessing: Beyond Recognition*. Minneapolis: University of Minnesota Press, 2001.

Pateman, Carol. *The Sexual Contract*. Standford University Press, 1988.